Praise for
Who Are the Real *Chosen People?*
The Meaning of Chosenness in Christianity, Judaism, and Islam

"With elegant concision and scrupulous fairness, Reuven Firestone has taken up the most contentious question in all of Western religious history and drawn off at least some of its poison. No teacher or serious student of the tangled relations among Judaism, Christianity, and Islam should be without this little book."
—**Jack Miles**, author, *God: A Biography*

"Rabbi Firestone takes us on a journey through the three monotheistic traditions of Judaism, Christianity, and Islam to uncover the meaning of 'chosenness.' He makes a compelling argument against parochial interpretations of this important concept, and illustrates how erroneously it has been associated with the self-exaltation of one religious community or another. This book is both informative and thought provoking."
—**Louay Safi, PhD**, executive director, Leadership Development Center, Islamic Society of North America

"With a rare depth and range of scholarly knowledge and theoretical sophistication as well as a sympathetic yet judicious eye, Reuven Firestone presents a portrait of the notion of chosenness in the three great Abrahamic Western religious traditions—Judaism, Christianity, and Islam—in a manner that is both magisterial and accessible. Scholars and laypeople, believers and skeptics alike will profit greatly from this informative and thought-provoking book."
—**Rabbi David Ellenson, PhD**, president, Hebrew Union College–Jewish Institute of Religion

"As we enter a new era of interreligious dialogue, the concept of 'chosenness' poses a serious problem. This is the first careful, fair, and thorough comparison of how the concept functions in the three major Abrahamic religions, all of which have their version of it. It will help move interreligious relations beyond the cliches in which it can sometimes become mired and into a needed honest grappling with the seemingly more intractable issues. It will be required reading for anyone interested in nurturing religious diversity in a globalizing world."
—**Harvey Cox**, Hollis Professor of Divinity, Harvard University

"Reuven Firestone has waded into the most troubled waters of interreligious conflict and navigated them fairly. This is a highly readable and well-balanced treatment of the tough issues—chosenness and exclusive claims—that have long marred the great moral achievements of montheism. A worthwhile sourcebook for all who participate in dialogue."
—**Dr. Arthur Green**, rector, Hebrew College Rabbinical School; author, *Seek My Face: A Jewish Mystical Theology* and *Ehyeh: A Kabbalah for Tomorrow*

"*Who Are the Real Chosen People?* raises a central discussion when examining the relationship between the three great Abrahamic faiths and interfaith dialogue. Rabbi Reuven Firestone has done the reader a favor by not glossing over the hard issues that confront us, rather offering a timely analysis of the concept of 'chosenness.' The reader needs to engage with Firestone's clear and sympathetic arguments in order to make sense of what is happening in the world today. Rabbi Firestone is truly a leader of moral courage and vision for our troubled times."
—**Akbar Ahmed, PhD**, Ibn Khaldun Chair of Islamic Studies, American University

"A fascinating topic and a highly stimulating exploration of chosenness in Judaism, Christianity, and Islam. Professor Firestone's research is thorough, and his discussion and conclusions provide much food for thought."
—**Ghada Osman, PhD**, director, Center for Islamic and Arabic Studies, San Diego State University

Who Are the *Real* Chosen People?

The Meaning of Chosenness in Judaism, Christianity and Islam

Reuven Firestone, PhD

Walking Together, Finding the Way®
SKYLIGHT PATHS® PUBLISHING
Woodstock, Vermont

Who Are the Real Chosen People?
The Meaning of Chosenness in Judaism, Christianity and Islam

2008 Hardcover Edition, First Printing
© 2008 by Reuven Firestone

Library of Congress Cataloging-in-Publication Data
Firestone, Reuven, 1952–
Who are the real chosen people? : the meaning of chosenness in Judaism, Christianity and Islam / Reuven Firestone.
p. cm. — (The center for religious inquiry series)
Includes bibliographical references and index.
ISBN-13: 978-1-59473-248-5 (hardcover)
ISBN-10: 1-59473-248-5 (hardcover)
 1. Salvation. 2. Election (Theology) 3. Monotheism. I. Title.
BL476.F57 2008
202'.2—dc22

10 9 8 7 6 5 4 3 2 1

Manufactured in the United States of America
Jacket design: Tim Holtz

Walking Together, Finding the Way®
Published by SkyLight Paths Publishing
A Division of Longhill Partners, Inc.
Sunset Farm Offices, Route 4, P.O. Box 237
Woodstock, VT 05091
Tel: (802) 457-4000   Fax: (802) 457-4004
www.skylightpaths.com

Contents

Introduction

The Language of Chosenness

Choosing is something we do every day, from our choice of what to wear in the morning to our decision at the end of the day to turn out the light rather than read that next chapter. Choosing is an ordinary act. We choose which seat we prefer on the bus, which route to take to work, which pen to use to write this paragraph. To choose is to select something freely and after consideration. When a person chooses, that person shows a preference for one thing over something else.

Choosing is also limiting. It is an act of identifying, of distinguishing, of separating. Although it is possible to choose "a few" rather than one, it is understood generally as singling out. The act of choosing immediately establishes a hierarchy. What is chosen is somehow different than the others. Usually, that difference represents a higher location on the ladder. It can also mean choosing a loser, of course, but that would be unintentional; when you make a choice, you hope you are choosing a winner. Being chosen, therefore, would appear to be a special and positive status that places the chosen over and above the non-chosen.

If being chosen is generally a good thing, consider being chosen by God.

Jews, Christians, and Muslims—all three families of monotheistic religions—claim in one way or another to be God's chosen community. Christian theologians have sometimes referred to God's choosing for special favor as "election." Whether called chosenness or election, the special nature of that divinely authorized status—its presumed superiority—has been glorified by religious civilizations when in positions of imperial power, and it has sustained religious communities suffering persecution. It has also made believers uncomfortable at times, especially in places where democracy, equality, and freedom are considered defining categories.

One important aspect of language is that every word has a range of meanings, often subtle, that affect its "personality." When we use a word in speech, we are often affected unconsciously by that word's subterranean tones and shades of meaning that have become associated with it through usage. The way a word has been used, say, in a famous speech or story provides shades of meaning that native speakers naturally pick up. Those nuances then enter the life of the word as it continues to be used in speech and in writing. This is very much the case with the word *chosen*. In his 1828 *American Dictionary of the English Language*, Noah Webster used biblical language to support most of his definitions. For his definition of *choose*, he includes, "To elect for eternal happiness; to predestinate to life." He cites Matthew 22:14, "Many are called but few chosen," and Mark 13:20, "For his elect's sake, whom he hath chosen."[1] This is a big jump from choosing between your beige or navy slacks.

To be chosen, then, can have a range of meaning from the mundane to the holy, but in all cases it means to be singled out and preferred over others. The criteria for having been chosen could vary, from size and gender to wisdom and experience, but in a deep sense that permeates much or most of Western culture (and conveyed by Webster's entry), having been chosen communicates a sense of something that is extraordinary, is transcendent, and entitles a reward. What is assumed in this sense of the term is that God has done the choosing and the reward is something that is unequaled, for what could possibly equal divinely ordained eternal happiness?

Those of us who live deeply within one of the three families of monotheism tend to accept the assumption of chosenness that is articulated within it at one level or another. It is good to believe that we live according to the will of God, and there is certainly nothing wrong about believing that we will receive divine reward for our religious activities or beliefs. For many of us, these beliefs represent deep and abiding aspects of who we are and what our purpose in life is. If we lived entirely within our religious communities and with no interaction with people of other faith traditions, we would most likely not give the notion of being chosen a second thought. But we live in a multireligious world and bump up against people and situations that sometimes challenge our religious assumptions. This is especially true when we hear believers in different faith traditions articulating the deep and abiding belief that *they* belong to God's chosen. That would imply that we do not. Can more than one be chosen? What about those of other faiths who seem so certain? Can a religious tradition that expects or requires different beliefs or behaviors than our own *also* represent God's will as surely as our own?

Unless we cut ourselves off entirely from interacting with anyone outside our religious communities, we cannot avoid this kind of cognitive dissonance. Knowing something about how and why the notion of chosenness has become so important in the monotheistic traditions can be useful because it can help us navigate between our own beliefs and those of others, and it can help us make sense of our own unique place in a complex world.

At some deep level there is a lot at stake in being chosen—or not being chosen. Webster's definition shows that chosenness is associated with scripture, with happiness and even eternal life, and with a divine sense of order. It remains for us to try to understand how and why the concept of preference for one person or people over others became so important in religion.

We will embark on this quest by traveling through the histories of emergence of Judaism, Christianity, and Islam and the early interaction between the believers in these religious traditions. And we will examine the scriptures of each as well. The translations of the Hebrew Bible and the Qur'an are my own, although I based them on well-respected English translations.[2] New Testament translations are derived from the Cambridge and Oxford Study Bibles.[3] In an attempt to preserve the original flavor of these works spanning thousands of years of history, the original sense of the language has been maintained whenever possible. This includes the use of masculine God language that may make some uncomfortable, but which I felt was necessary given the nature of this study.

1

In the Beginning ...

"In the beginning God created the heavens and the earth" (Gen. 1:1). Divine creation did not privilege one set of objects or beings over another. All were created from the word of God, and before the creation of humanity on the sixth day, all things were "created equal"—the heavens and the earth and all that are in them.

The language of creation is consistent. "Let there be ... And so it was!" The sound of the Hebrew words for these phrases is airy and breathy, with the accent on the last syllable: *Yehi! ... Vayehi!* The very act of creation conveys a feeling of breath in Hebrew, of breathing. Breath is life; when God said *Yehi* (Be!), God was breathing life into creation. That very same Hebrew root for the act of creation is the root that forms the name of God, a name that Jews have not pronounced for thousands of years out of respect for the divine countenance. The meaning of those unpronounceable sounds is "the One-Who-Is." The very name of God thus conveys the sense of the breath of life, the energy that powers the world and all that is in it. Later, when Moses asked God to tell him the divine name, God answered, *"Ehyeh asher ehyeh,"* which loosely translates to "I am the becoming," or "I am what is."

The language of creation continues through the creation of all aspects of life and the world. "God said, 'Let there be light,' and there

1

was light" (Gen.1:3). "God said, 'Let there be a firmament between the waters … and so it was" (1:6–7). This language continues through the creation of the two platforms for living things: the waters and the earth. God commands the waters and the earth to produce living things, and they do: first plants, and then swarming things, flying things, swimming things, creeping things. God makes all the various categories of animals. Then the language of creation changes.

"God said, 'Let us make human beings in our image, after our likeness, to have dominion over the fish in the sea, the birds of the air, the cattle, all wild animals on land, and everything that creeps on the earth'" (Gen. 1:26). This verse has stimulated more commentary than perhaps any other verse in the entire Bible because it raises so many questions about the nature of God and the nature of humanity. We are concerned here with only a tiny piece of the mystery, and that is the narrowing of focus from all of creation to only one small piece of it: humankind.

From that instant onward, the biblical epic history of the universe is focused only on one miniscule part of that universe. Other parts of the world move in and out of focus only as they impact the history of humanity. That point is made quite clearly in the very next chapter, when the details of God's creation of humanity and the story of the Garden of Eden are prefaced with the words, "This is the story of the heavens and the earth after their creation" (Gen. 2:4).

Surprisingly enough, "the story of the heavens and the earth after their creation" tells us virtually nothing about the heavens and the earth. What it *does* tell us is all about the history of humanity, from Adam and Eve and Cain and Abel to the generations leading to Noah and his family, the Tower of Babel, and finally, Abraham.

We can think of the universal narrative of the Hebrew Bible[1] like the beginning of some films that open with a wide-angle shot that takes in the world in which the story takes place. That large picture soon narrows and eventually focuses on the heroes of the story. But unlike films that use this technique (a technique that may have been borrowed unconsciously from the core narrative that the Bible represents for the West), the Bible does it twice. The first is the focus from creation to the story of humanity. The second is the focus from the story of all humanity to the story of one tiny family within it.

Why the double focus? That narrowing technique makes you come away from the biblical story of humankind with the impression that it was a failed experiment. The narrative structure of the first chapter of Genesis reveals that God's primary concern with creation was the formation of that set of creatures that is referenced as being constructed somehow in the divine image. Exactly what "divine image" means is open to interpretation, but the first four stories of the Bible that follow creation demonstrate the consistent failure of humanity to live up to that image and God's expectation. Adam and Eve failed God in the Garden of Eden (Genesis 3). Cain committed the unforgivable crime of fratricide (Gen. 4:1–16). Noah's entire generation was deeply steeped in violence (Gen. 6:9–13), and the builders of the Tower of Babel conspired to build a structure that would reach the heavens only for the purpose of self-aggrandizement (Gen. 11:1–9).

In each story, humanity was left alone to fend for itself in the new and glorious world that God had created. Each time, humanity failed, and in every case God articulated heavenly disapproval through words and punishments. Why did humanity always fail when it had all the privileges? Humans were given dominion over the fish in the sea, the birds of the air, the cattle, all wild animals on land, and everything that creeps on the earth. And yet they failed repeatedly to realize their potential represented by that mysterious likeness of God.

God's last act of disapproval resulted in the dispersion of humanity after the fiasco of the Tower of Babel. From that point on, the divine modus operandi changes radically. God would no longer simply leave humanity to go it alone. From that moment onward in the Bible's narrative history of humankind, God would intervene in human history and not wait for another failure. God would henceforth engage personally with humanity—but not with all of humanity. The scale would be narrowed down to one individual and that individual's family.

It was almost as if God took one small sample from the whole and conducted an experiment. What would happen if God personally engaged in a relationship with one person from that mass of problematic creation called humankind? How would things fare if God informed and instructed that person and encouraged the behavior that humankind proved incapable of doing on its own? The experiment was conducted with Abraham and with his immediate family. God chose Abraham.

A New Modus Operandi

God's choice of Abraham is mysterious in the Hebrew Bible. No reason is provided for that fateful call when God suddenly spoke and said, "Leave your country, your kin, and your father's house, and go to a land that I will show you" (Gen. 12:1). God establishes a covenant with Abraham in Genesis 17. A covenant is like a contract or an agreement, and in the agreement established in Genesis 17, God promises to fulfill the promises made to him earlier: that Abraham would be a great nation (Gen. 12:2; in Gen. 17 God promises that Abraham would be the father of many nations) and that he would possess the land of Canaan. For his part, Abraham was required to "live always in [God's] presence."

The Hebrew original of this phrase is very important: *"Hithalekh lefanay veheyeh tamim"* (Gen. 17:1). This short phrase is often translated in a way that does not quite capture its essence. "Live always in My presence and be blameless" (RSV), and "Walk in My ways and be blameless" (New JPS), do not convey the conditional sense of the phrase. A better translation would be, "If you walk in my ways, you will be blameless," or, "Walk in my ways in order to be blameless."

What's the difference? The conditional sense of the phrase is critical because it conveys that God is promising a reward for human engagement with the Divine. Life in the semidesert environments of the ancient Near East was always precarious. Drought, famine, disease, enemy attack, accidents, infertility, and a host of other incidents could easily spell disaster for a man and his family. In the ancient world, adverse incidents such as these were often understood as punishments brought on by the gods. Reward and punishment in the ancient Near East occurred in this world. There is no evidence until the last chapter of the book of Daniel, the latest book of the Hebrew Bible, that biblical people believed in an afterlife in which the righteous would be rewarded or the sinful would be punished. In the worldview conveyed by the Hebrew Bible, reward and punishment were meted out entirely in this world. God was therefore giving Abraham the following message: "If you live in my presence by walking in my ways and living according to my will, you will be innocent of any kinds of sins or errors that would bring on divine punishment in the form of famine or accidents or infertility." God promises to protect Abraham and make him into a great nation (Gen. 12:2); indeed, Abraham will be the father of many nations (Gen. 17:5). Abraham's offspring will be greater than the sands on the seashore (Gen. 22:17) or the stars in heaven (Gen. 15:5). His name will be great and he will be a blessing (Gen. 12:2). All the nations of the earth shall bless themselves through him (Gen. 12:3).

"Just respond to my intervention," God is telling Abraham. "I will be there for you, but you must also be there for me!" This, then, is God's new modus operandi. No longer aloof as in the first eleven chapters of Genesis, God begins in chapter 12 to engage personally with Abraham and the biblical patriarchs and matriarchs. God guides this Abrahamic family, gives warnings and blessings, and provides a sense of purpose and design to human life. In short, God commands and the Abrahamic family obeys.

There is, of course, room for maneuver. God expects obedience but does not demand that Abraham give up free will. The human party to the covenant always retains his own freedom to choose, so Abraham and his family continue to struggle in the world, even under the protection of God. Sarah and Hagar struggle over their status as rival wives to Abraham, each with her own son contending for primary (or chosen) status that would result in greater inheritance and blessing in the next generation. Abraham naturally becomes involved in those conflicts (Genesis 16, 17, 21), and eventually needs to make a decision about how they will be resolved.

Abraham demonstrates his own personal initiative when he argues with God over the fate of the inhabitants of Sodom and Gomorra (Gen. 18:20–32). The stories of Abraham exemplify the patriarchal narratives of the Hebrew Bible, which display humans making decisions, and the sometimes questionable results of those decisions. But they also portray God as available for guidance when necessary and sometimes directly intervening.

The Bible's narrowing of the focus to Abraham is forceful and clear. Abraham represents God's new operating method, a new possibility of human relationship with God and the divine blessing. The new method is covenantal and total, and it brought Abraham enormous benefit. Abraham, therefore, becomes symbolic in the Bible for that most elite existential position: being God's chosen one. Abraham was the first monotheist. He was the recipient of God's repeated blessing. And God loved Abraham as God loved no other. In the entire Bible, Abraham is the only person represented as God's love, God's friend; he is called *avraham ohavi* (Abraham, My love) (Isa. 41:8).

What about the rest of humanity? Where are they once the camera has focused on the family of Abraham? From the end of the story of the Tower of Babel in Genesis 11 onward, the Bible rarely references humanity as a whole. Parts of humanity enter into the picture only as they come into contact with the Abrahamic family and its offspring. After the narrowing of the story to the choice of Abraham, the great history that began as the story of humanity becomes a history of humanity through the story of the Abrahamic family. But that tiny family grows and becomes more significant in its relations with the rest of the world, expanding over a few generations from a nuclear family to an extended family, a clan, a tribe, and then a nation.

The Mystery of the Divine Choice

God's choice of Abraham was neither the first nor the last time that God made a mysterious choice. The first was when God accepted

Abel's offering from his flocks but did not accept Cain's offering from his cultivation (Genesis 4). No reason for that fateful choice is given. Despite the brief intervention of warning Cain about his anger and resentment, God does not engage in any consistent relationship with that generation. God simply favored one brother over the other in a mysterious manner that remains open to interpretation to this day.

In the generation after Abraham, God chose only one of the patriarch's two sons to be the bearer of the divine covenant (Gen. 17:15–21). The reason for the divine choice of Isaac is again mysterious, although Ishmael was not rejected entirely. He received a divine blessing that was not insignificant, but he was also removed from the ongoing history of humanity as narrated in the Bible (Gen. 17:19–21).

In the following generation, Jacob becomes the chosen one. The choice is less obvious but also less mysterious because Jacob demonstrates his own initiative in obtaining the birthright that was due to be given to his older brother, Esau (Gen. 25:29–34). He is also maneuvered into position to receive his father's blessing through the initiative of his mother (Gen. 27:1–40). But the decision of who will be God's chosen one is not left only to human actions; God blesses only Jacob (Gen. 28:10–15, 35:9–12), who then fathers twelve sons who will represent the twelve tribes of Israel. Like Ishmael, his uncle (and father-in-law!) before him, Esau drops out of human history, and his descendents enter and exit the scene only when they have an impact on the history of the tribes of Israel.

Jacob's name is changed to Israel when he receives his own divine blessings (first in Gen. 32:29 and again in Gen. 35:10). Human history in the Bible then becomes the history of a clan of brothers whose numbers of offspring grow into a loose tribal confederation after moving to Egypt. Finally, after experiencing a population explosion under Egyptian slavery (Exodus 1) and redemption from slavery and oppression through God's power and grace (Exod. 3–15), the tribal confederation becomes unified into a nation by the experience of a renewed covenant with God at the foot of Mount Sinai.

On the third new moon after the Israelites had gone forth from the land of Egypt ... Moses went up to God. The Lord called to him from the mountain, saying: "Thus shall you say to the house of Jacob and declare to the children of Israel: 'You have seen what I did to the Egyptians, how I bore you on eagles' wings and brought you to Me. Now then, if you will obey Me conscientiously and keep My covenant, you shall be My treasured possession among all the peoples, for all the earth is Mine, and you shall be to Me a kingdom of priests and a holy nation.'" (Exod. 19:1, 3–6)

This renewed covenant marks another change in the mode of divine engagement with God's chosen people. The book of Exodus counts the number of those who marched out of Egypt by tallying the men of fighting age. The number given in Exodus 12:37 and Numbers 11:21 is six hundred thousand men of fighting age. Adjusting for gender and age, that would equal a total of some two million Israelites who came together to receive the renewed covenant at Mount Sinai. We must add to this number a mixed multitude of other oppressed peoples who escaped with the Israelites from Egypt (Exod. 12:37–38). The total number would have been simply too many people for personal, individual engagement with God, so the model of covenant used with the patriarchs and matriarchs was updated. Now the system would be one of divine intervention through the enactment of clear rules of behavior established by God. Henceforth, God's chosen human experiment would be governed by the rule of law.

Moses went and repeated to the people all the commands of the Lord and all the rules; and all the people answered with one voice, saying, "All the things that the Lord has commanded we will do!" Moses then wrote down all the commands of the Lord. Early in the morning, he set up an altar at the foot of the mountain, with twelve pillars for the twelve tribes of Israel. He designated some young men among the Israelites, and they offered burnt offerings and sacrificed bulls as offerings of well-being to the Lord. Moses took one part of the blood and put it in basins, and the other part of the blood he dashed against the altar. Then he took the Book of the Covenant and read it aloud to the people. And they said, "All that the Lord has spoken, we will conscientiously do!" Moses took the blood and dashed it on the people and said, "This is the blood of the covenant which the Lord now makes with you concerning all these commands." (Exod. 24:3–8)

The dashing of the blood of the covenant on the people was both a ritual and a legal act. It was a way for the people in a preliterate society to commit publicly in a manner that parallels large numbers of people signing a petition today. This act, along with their open declaration of acceptance ("All that the Lord has spoken, we will conscientiously do!"), was a formal public pronouncement that Israel would try to abide by the terms of the covenant now defined by a code of behavior. From that moment onward, the chosen nature of the divine relationship would apply not simply to an individual or a family, but to a nation. Comprised of a combination of ethnic kin through Jacob's genealogical line and a mix of fellow escapees representing various ethnic histories, this new covenanted, chosen people would henceforth be called "Israel."[2]

The Hebrew Bible subsequently would not mince words in its depiction of Israel's uniqueness and chosen relationship with God:

- And you shall be holy to Me, for I the Lord am holy, and I have set you apart from other peoples to be Mine (Lev. 20:26).
- For you are a people consecrated to the Lord your God: of all the peoples of the earth the Lord your God chose you to be His treasured people (Deut. 7:6).

- For you are a people consecrated to the Lord your God: the Lord your God chose you from among all other peoples on earth to be His treasured people (Deut. 14:2).
- I the Lord, in My grace, have summoned you, and I have grasped you by the hand. I created you, and appointed you a covenant people, a light of nations (Isa. 42:6).
- Hear now, O Jacob My servant, Israel whom I have chosen (Isa. 44:1)!
- You alone have I singled out [known] of all the families of the earth (Amos 3:2).
- Happy is the nation whose God is the Lord, the people He has chosen to be His own (Ps. 33:12).
- For the Lord has chosen Jacob for Himself, Israel, as His treasured possession (Ps. 135:4).

Here we face one of the greatest conundrums to challenge those who count the Hebrew Bible to be divine (or divinely inspired) scripture. Although God created all humanity in the divine likeness, why is one community of God's loving creatures privileged over all the others? Even with humanity's repeated failures to live up to that likeness without ongoing heavenly intervention, why would a loving God not find a way to allow all of humankind to benefit directly from engagement with the Divine? We can uncover some important information about this by examining the biblical notion of chosenness as it fits into the ancient Near Eastern world out of which biblical religion emerged.

2

Chosenness in the Ancient Near East

The Ancient Near Eastern Context

Ancient Near East is a slippery term because it overlaps with other terms such as *Middle East, Fertile Crescent,* and *Mesopotamia.* The area of the ancient Near East corresponds roughly with that of today's eastern Mediterranean, from Greece in the west to Iran in the east, and Turkey in the north to Arabia and Egypt in the south. This area includes today's countries of Turkey, Syria, Lebanon, Israel, Palestine, Egypt, Jordan, Arabia, and Iraq. The time period of the ancient Near East ranges from as early as we have record until the cultural penetration of Greece and then Rome in the third century BCE. All the monotheistic religions find their roots in the cultures, languages, and religious ideas of the ancient Near East.

In this ancient human environment, the world and nature were understood to function under the powers of deities. Some of those deities had special jurisdiction over parts of nature, such as the weather, the waters, or the fertility of crops and herds. Others had special jurisdiction over groups of people organized around kinship. In the ancient Near East, national groups were organized through large kinship networks. Members of tribal nations belonged to nuclear families, which functioned as parts of larger extended family clans, which in turn were parts of much larger extended kinship groups that we call tribes. As in the case of biblical Israel, related tribes made up a "nation" or a people, and in the ancient Near East, every national unit seems to have had its own national goddess or god.

There were other divine powers besides the national god, but each nation had a unique relationship with its "own" god. If you were a Moabite, for example, your national god was Kemosh. Kemosh protected you and your kin. He would also make sure your crops and your flocks were fertile, and protect you and your family and tribe from attack by foreigners. In return, you made offerings to him and demonstrated your loyalty and that of your family to him.

The gods of other nations would normally take no interest in you, nor you in them. Born a Moabite, you were born into a community that worshiped its Moabite god, Kemosh. You could no easier change gods or religions than you could change your family history. Nevertheless, if you were in a foreign land, you would most likely make an offering to the local god as a form of respect and a means of gaining needed temporary protection in the area under the god's jurisdiction. Because there were many deities that powered the world, you might wish to hedge your bets and make sure that offerings were made to certain foreign gods as well as your own national deity even when not traveling.

One particular feature of religious life in the ancient Near East is that all believers were "chosen" by their national gods. While believing in other divine powers that inhabited sacred areas or protected other peoples, every nation had its own exclusive relationship with its own national god. The god of the Hebrew Bible is sometimes called the "God of Israel" (Gen. 33:20), but it also had a personal name, like all the other gods. As mentioned in chapter 1, that name conveyed a meaning similar to "being" or "existence."

Although the name was no doubt pronounced at one time, its articulation was eventually forbidden. The reason for this prohibition is probably associated with issues of relationship and power. If you know someone's name, you have a certain advantage, even power, over them, particularly if they do not know yours. Most of us remember being at a gathering where we bump into someone who knew our name while we didn't remember or know his or hers; the lack of balance in the relationship made us uncomfortable. I once wore a T-shirt with my name on it as a young boy. When I walked past a couple of boys my age whom I didn't know, they read my name and then called out, "Hey, Reuven!" They knew my name, but I didn't know theirs. Not only did I feel quite silly, but I also felt vulnerable. Somehow, knowing my name gave them a decided advantage over me. I felt as if they had the upper hand in the relationship, and it made me feel anxious and uncomfortable. Only later did I figure out that this feeling relates to the sense of power associated with knowing a name. In some traditional societies, people change the name of sick children in order to confuse the angel of death or demon who might take the child. Without knowing the child's name, the demon doesn't have the power to take him or her.

In polytheistic systems, humans try to influence the gods through persuasion or manipulation—sometimes even through magic. In the polytheism practiced in the ancient Near East, people knew the names of their gods and used the names for this persuasion and manipulation. But in monotheism there is only one great Creator-God, the one all-powerful God of all. Humans could not possibly have the power or strength to manipulate the awesome God of all creation. It therefore became strange to refer to the One Great God by a personal name.

Biblical scholars agree that the Israelites once related to their God of Israel like other tribal nations related to their own national gods. Each god had a name and each was limited in power. But the Israelites made the transition from polytheism to monotheism, and the God of Israel transformed in the eyes of the Israelites to become the God of the entire universe. Although God did not change, the human *conception* of God changed during this transition period. So the once-named god became known as "the Lord" or simply, "God"—the source of being, the all. After that transition occurred, it seemed impossible for humans to pronounce God's name. Keep in mind also that in the old polytheistic religions, knowing and uttering a god's name was thought to release some of its power. With that notion in the background, uttering the name of the One Great God might endanger the entire community by releasing some of God's unlimited power. That notion seemed to linger among the ancient Israelites, so it evolved into the belief that you would have to be extremely powerful and protected in order to mention God's name without being consumed by the very force that might be released.

While the Jerusalem Temple was still standing, ancient Israel had a ritual ceremony in which the name of God was actually uttered, but this was done in a carefully controlled manner. In fact, according to the second-century book of Jewish tradition called the Mishnah (Yoma 6:2), it actually became an annual ritual requirement that took place on the most sacred day in the calendar, Yom Kippur (the Day of Atonement). This most sacred utterance of the divine name could be pronounced only on the holiest day of the year. It had to be pronounced in the most sacred location on earth—the inner sanctum of the Jerusalem Temple, known as the *Kodesh Kodashim* (the Holy of Holies). And it could be uttered only by the most highly consecrated individual on earth—the high priest, who had to endure a period of careful physical and spiritual preparation in order to attain the required state of absolute ritual purity. According to rabbinic tradition, a rope was tied around the high priest's ankle in the event that he was not properly prepared, ritually and spiritually, for the uttering of the divine name. If he failed, he would be burned up within the Holy of Holies and his body could only be retrieved by having it dragged out. In the event of such a catastrophe, a second high priest went through the same preparatory process in order to be prepared to utter the divine name in his place.

So the pronunciation of the name of the God of Israel became forbidden and eventually lost.[1] But for centuries before the transition to monotheism, the "God of Israel" was exactly that—limited to the Israelites (see Exod. 5:1, for example). As noted, the Moabites who lived next to Israelites, in the hill country to the east (today's central Jordan), had their own national deity named Kemosh (Num. 21:29). North of the Moabites were the Ammonites, whose national god was Milkom (1 Kings 11:6). The Philistines, who lived on the plain to the west of ancient Israel between today's Gaza and Tel Aviv, had Dagon as their god (1 Sam. 5), and further up the coast, the inhabitants of Tyre had a goddess named Ashtoret (2 Kings 23:13). Each ethnic community had a unique relationship with its god. They were "chosen" for each other. The god protected its community, provided for it, and fought for it. In return, it was worshiped and offerings were made to it.

In the ancient world, the normal tensions that arose between ethnic or national communities were often mirrored by tension between their gods. An oracle to King Esarhaddon, who ruled the Assyrian Empire from 680 to 669 BCE,[2] demonstrates the protector role not only of the gods, but also of the goddesses. The god's personal name was always given to identify the specific source of the power: "Esarhaddon, king of the lands, fear not! That wind which blows against you—I need only say a word and I can bring it to an end. Your enemies, like a young boar in the month of Simanu, will flee even at your approach. I am the great Belet—I am the goddess Ishtar of Arbela, she who has destroyed your enemies at your mere approach."[3] Wars between nations may have been fought by tribal soldiers, but victory or defeat was determined by national gods. Wars were won or lost according to the fighters' ability to please their gods.

The God of Israel was assumed to have fought along with the Israelite people in their own wars. In the victory song intoned after the defeat of Pharaoh's armies in the Red Sea, God is praised as *ish milchamah* (the warrior; literally, "Man of War," Exod. 15:3). And when Israel is preparing to conquer the land of Canaan under God's direction, they are reassured:

When you take the field against your enemies and see horses
and chariots—forces larger than yours—have no fear of
them for the Lord your God who brought you from the land
of Egypt is with you.... Do not be in fear or in panic or in
dread of them, for it is the Lord your God who marches
with you to do battle for you against your enemy, to bring
you victory! (Deut. 20:1–4)

We must keep in mind that the Hebrew word that is translated
as "Lord" is actually the four letters that make up the "personal
name" of the God of Israel. "Lord your God" in this passage orig-
inally would be rendered by God's personal name, followed by the
description, "your God," so the reassurance was given in the actual
name of Israel's own national deity.

The Hebrew Bible contains a number of stories that demonstrate the special relationship of a god with its people in time of
war. One particularly interesting example is a war between the
Moabites and the Israelites. This story is especially important
because it is recorded both in the Bible, in 2 Kings 3, and in another
ancient Near Eastern text, a stone monument called the Mesha
Stele (or Moabite Stone). The Mesha Stele is an ancient basalt
tablet written for the Moabite king Mesha in about 850 BCE; it
was written in Moabite, a language so close to Hebrew that they
can be understood as dialects of the same language. It records the
same story found in 2 Kings, but from the Moabite perspective.
The two sources tell us that the war actually happened, but provide
two conflicting versions of the outcome. In the following two versions
of the story, if you substitute an actual divine name for "the Lord"
in the Bible version, or if you subtitute "the Lord" for the name
Kemosh in the Mesha version, you can see how similar the styles of
the two versions are.

According to the Bible, the Moabites were weaker than the
Israelites and had fallen under Israelite rule. As a result, they
paid heavy taxes to Israel. But the king of Israel "did evil in the
sight of the Lord," for which the God of Israel allowed the

Moabite king Mesha to rebel. In response, the Israelites assembled a coalition of three kings with their armies and set out to reconquer the Moabites. They expected to find water in a certain ravine to resupply their troops near the field of battle, but found the water source to be dry. This became a key issue in the battle that followed.

"Alas!" cried the king of Israel. "The Lord has brought these three kings together only to deliver them into the hands of Moab!" But when the Israelite leaders consulted a prophet of God to determine whether God would support them, the prophet went into an oracular trance and proclaimed, "Thus says the Lord: This ravine shall be full of pools. For thus said the Lord: You shall see no wind, you shall see no rain, and yet the ravine shall be filled with water; and you and your cattle and your pack animals shall drink. And this is but a slight thing in the sight of the Lord, for He will also deliver Moab into your hands" (2 Kings 3:10–18).

As the holy man prophesied, water began to flow and the Israelites were refreshed. The Moabites were then tricked into attacking the Israelite camp but were routed. The Israelites overpowered all the Moabite cities and pushed the remaining army into the walled city of Kir Hareshet. Things did not get any better for the Moabites there. They became trapped behind the walls of their own fortress when they failed in their attempt to send a column for help. In desperation, King Mesha sacrificed his own son as a burnt offering. Suddenly, after that sacrifice, the Israelites withdrew and the story ends.

It is not clear from the biblical text exactly what happened as a result of the sacrifice. The literal translation of the Hebrew is, "So [King Mesha] took his firstborn son, who was to succeed him as king, and offered him up on the wall as a burnt offering. A great wrath came upon Israel, so they withdrew from him and returned to [their own] land" (2 Kings 3:27).

The Mesha Stele tells a different version of the story. According to this version written by King Mesha, the king of Israel "oppressed Moab for many days":

for [the Moabite god] Kemosh was angry with his land.... But Kemosh restored it in my days ... the king of Israel built [the city of] Atarot for himself, and I fought against the city and captured it. And I killed all the people of the city as a sacrifice for Kemosh and for Moab. And I brought back the fire-hearth of his uncle from there; and I brought it before the face of Kemosh in Qeriot ... and Kemosh said to me, "Go, take [the city of] Nebo from Israel." And I went in the night and fought against it from the daybreak until midday, and I took it and I killed the whole population ... and from there I took the vessels of YHWH [the four-letter name of the Israelite god preserved in the stone tablet], and I presented them before the face of Kemosh. And the king of Israel had built [the city of] Yahaz, and he stayed there throughout his campaign against me; and Kemosh drove him away before my face.

Each version of this story has a particular point of view and tells the tale as a partisan advocate. There is clearly no interest or attempt to offer a neutral report, but it is clear that from the perspective of each side, it is the relationship with the national god that is key to winning wars. The Bible often relates to the God of Israel from a parochial perspective, though as the notion of the God of Israel expanded to the notion of a single God of the entire world, the perspective changes. Some biblical texts depict a global perspective where, for example, the God of Israel destroys all the gods of the Egyptians: "I shall execute judgment, I the Lord, against all the gods of Egypt" (Exod. 12:12). In others, God uses the Assyrians or Babylonians as a tool to punish Israel when it is sinful, even to the extent of destroying the northern kingdom of Israel by the hand of Assyria (2 Kings 17). By the time God is understood in purely monotheistic terms, the gods of Babylonia or other competing nations no longer figure in the narrative. They have dropped out because they are no longer considered to exist.

Choosing Religion

Because Israel seems to have been the only community to make the transition from polytheism to monotheism in this period, it saw itself situated in a world of many errant nations that were engaged in the worship of false gods. In such a religious environment where a person naturally remained loyal to his or her ethnic religion and national deity, Israel remained loyal to the "God of Israel," whom they also saw as the God of the entire universe. Even (or perhaps especially) after the transition to monotheism, absolute loyalty to their God became critical. Disloyalty did not mean simply abandoning one god for another, for that was impossible. In their world, disloyalty meant continuing to hedge their bets as in the old polytheistic world, when the God of Israel was understood to be the one and only God of the universe. It meant making offerings to other powers *in addition* to worshiping the One Great God, the God of Israel.

We can imagine the enormity of difference between Israelite religion and the religious practices of all its neighbors if we think about all the various ethno-religious communities of the ancient Near East as practicing one overarching religion. The Moabites and the Ammonites and the Kenites and the Jebusites may have worshiped different gods, but they all followed the same basic assumptions about how those gods functioned and how religion worked. They were all practicing the same religion even if their worship was directed toward different deities. Israel was the only community that practiced according to a different religious concept.

It might appear odd that the Israelites did not proselytize. Although the Bible records how the transition from polytheism to monotheism took time and was sometimes rocky (see, for example, all the polytheistic practices that were removed from Jerusalem by King Josiah in 2 Kings 23:4–15), the Israelites eventually became confident in their monotheism and deeply faithful to God. Yet, it seems they did not try to bring the "good news" to others steeped in the falsity of idolatry. This may seem strange from our perspective, but the truth of the matter is that mission was not really a possibility in those days. The religious environment of the ancient Near East was radically different from ours today, where religions openly compete with one another for members in a "free market" of religions. In the ancient world of ethnic religion, it was simply impossible to abandon your national god. In those days, the notion that you could believe or disbelieve in a religion was not a conceptual option. The world was perceived as functioning according to the divine powers that ran it, and there was no possibility to even conceive of something different.[4]

In fact, the notion that you could scope out religious options and choose the one that made most sense was not a conceptual possibility in the Near East until the Greeks imported the notion through their interest in philosophy. It was the Greeks who developed philosophical schools, each of which offered a different way of making sense of the world. In the great Greek cities, you could attend various schools, learn their philosophies, and then consider which to subscribe to. These were philosophies rather than religions, but it was simple enough for people to apply the notion of deciding which *philosophical* system made most sense to which *religious* system made most sense. This idea would not come to the land of Israel, however, until later. Before the Greeks brought Hellenism with them from within the borders of Hellas to the rest of the Near East, religious affiliation was a national affair.

The God of Israel had been understood by Israelites in the early period of their history to be a tribal god parallel to the tribal gods of neighboring peoples. Israel's god was (hopefully) more powerful than the other gods, as seems to be the sense of Exodus 15:16: "Lord, who is like You among the gods? Who is like You, majestic in holiness, worthy of awe and praise, worker of wonders?" (see also Exod. 12:12, Num. 33:4). But in the early period, the God of Israel functioned very much like the gods of the neighboring peoples, the "gods of the nations" (Ps. 96:5).

For some reason or reasons that remain matters of debate among theologians and historians of religion alike, religious ideas began to change among the Israelites. This seismic shift seems to have occurred during the period of the great classical prophets (roughly, the eighth to sixth centuries BCE). The prophets insisted that the God of Israel was also the God of the entire universe. By the time of Isaiah, Jeremiah, and Ezekiel, Israelite religion held firmly that the God of Israel was actually the *only* God: "I am the Lord, and there is none other; apart from Me there is no god" (Isa. 45:5).[5]

The Emergence of Monotheism

Although it is perhaps surprising, Israel was not the only community to have arrived at the notion of monotheism, and it may not have been the first. Other monotheisms or proto-monotheisms, such as that of the Egyptian pharaoh Akhenaten, may have existed for a limited time, but they could not be sustained.[6] Israel was the only community that successfully held on to this view in the ancient Near East. Because it was the lone monotheist community, it was constantly on the defensive in a world full of enticements to engage in worship of foreign gods (Num. 25:1–9; 2 Kings 23:4–15).

Once the God of Israel was known as the God of the universe, it became absolutely forbidden to engage in any activity that smacked of worshiping other gods. The old habit of hedging your bets by making offerings to other deities or powers in nature became strictly forbidden. Infidelity to the God of Israel is referred to in the Bible as straying after or worshiping other gods (Exod. 20:2, 23:13; Deut. 5:6, 6:14, 11:16; Jer. 1:16, 7:6). The transition to monotheism, however, was neither smooth nor total. Not everyone in the Israelite community was completely convinced that the old, premonotheistic Israelite religious practices of its earliest days were necessarily false or useless. The emergence of monotheism seems to have been a process, and the Bible itself is witness to movements to ban polytheism and countermovements to reestablish it. As noted above, a partial menu of the kinds of polytheistic practices that were available to ancient Israel can be seen in 2 Kings 23:4–15, a chapter that details King Josiah's religious reforms. It mentions many of the old practices by listing all the popular and varied types of polytheistic worship that Josiah destroyed. He smashed the objects made for the Canaanite gods, Ba'al and Asherah and the Host of heaven, he suppressed the idolatrous priests throughout the land who made offerings to Ba'al and to the sun and moon and constellations. He tore down the cubicles of the male religious prostitutes that were situated within the Temple itself, and destroyed many altars and shrines, including the Tofeth in Gey Ben-Hinnom, where people sacrificed their children (they "passed their sons or daughters through fire") to Molekh.[7] He also destroyed the horses dedicated to the sun and burned the chariots of the sun, defiled shrines built for the goddess Ashtoret and the god Kemosh on the Mount of the Destroyer, and shattered the sacred pillars and posts.

According to the direction of current biblical scholarship, these were not all merely foreign deities, the gods of the hated Canaanites. Some were actually gods traditionally worshiped by Israel. Biblical scholars such as Niels Peter Lemche have shown that *Canaan* refers more to a geographical area than a people, a land in which lived a variety of peoples that we know from biblical texts as Hittites, Girgashites, Emorites, Perizites, Hivites, and the like, often lumped together in the Bible (and Egyptian and Mesopotamian texts) as Canaanites.[8] The Israelites lived there, too.

Israel, it now appears, may have actually emerged as a distinct people out of the land called Canaan. According to many scholars of the Bible today (and putting it bluntly), Israelites *were* Canaanites, but they were one courageous group of Canaanites that was moving in the direction of an innovative religious idea that was becoming what we would later call monotheism. The Bible itself witnesses the bumpy road to the realization of that religious idea.

In the system articulated in the Hebrew Bible, responsibility to follow the revealed will of God found in the Torah is not a universal responsibility. It is directed specifically to Israel. It may seem strange to us that a religion espousing a concept of a universal God would appear to be unconcerned about the religious welfare and practices of those situated outside the receiving group, but recall that in the ancient Near East, religion was by definition distinctively ethnic. Each ethnic or national group had its own god or pantheon, and each national god had a unique relationship with its ethnic community. The God of Israel may have become conceptualized as the one and universal God that created and now powers the heavens and the earth, but it was intimately known as the God of Israel, and it retained that distinctive relationship with its people. It would simply seem strange to Israelite and non-Israelite alike for this tribal organization of monotheists to try to convince other tribal organizations to abandon their gods for the God of Israel.

On the other hand, because of Israel's unique position as the only monotheist community in the ancient Near East, intermarriage with peoples professing other religions was strictly forbidden. Such intermingling was liable to distract from the austere practices of monotheism among a small group living in a world of many peoples and nations, each associated with colorful, multiple deities and enticing worship rituals. The Moabites and Midianites seem to have been two of the biggest threats to Israel in this regard, and God warns Israel repeatedly not to follow the whims—or the women—of these neighboring peoples (Numbers 25).

Aside from the Israelites, however, intermarriage between peoples representing different religions may not have represented a significant theological problem in the polytheistic ancient Near East. If you traveled across national boundaries, you would pass from place to place but often find very similar gods. Those gods might have had different names, but they were easily recognizable by strangers because they occupied a similar or identical place on what you might call "the food chain of divinity."

In virtually every ethno-religious system, for example, there was a god associated with fertility. That god may have different names in different places, but its job description was just about the same everywhere. Among the Israelites, on the other hand, one God was understood to control all aspects of nature and time, and Israel was permitted to worship only this one God, this "zealous god" (Exod. 20:4, 34:14; Deut. 4:24, 5:8, 15), who would tolerate no confusion or association with other deities. Intermarriage with people who worshiped their own national gods was always a threat to the unity and survival of this one small community. Even with those groups such as the Egyptians and Edomites, among whom the Israelites were permitted by biblical scripture to marry, intermarriage was allowed only after three generations of the foreigners had assimilated into the Israelite cultural and religious system (Deut. 23:8–9).

Israel was only one small ethno-religious people among the many peoples and religions of the ancient world. According to the sentiment expressed repeatedly in the Bible, Israelite religious leaders felt the stress of the theological insistence on monotheism in a world of multiple deities. Some neighboring religious systems, for example, had enticing ritual practices such as sacred prostitution, most likely human sympathetic acts of public coitus in order to stimulate the gods to do the same and thus provide fertility to their people's pastoral or agricultural economies (1 Kings 14:24; Hos. 4:12–19; Ezek. 23:5–10). As Deuteronomy articulates the relationship,

> [Many nations] ... will draw your children away from the Lord to serve other gods ... for you are a people holy to the Lord your God, and He has chosen you out of all peoples on earth to be His special possession. It is not because you are more numerous than any other nation that the Lord cared for you and chose you, for you are the smallest of all nations; it was because the Lord loved you and stood by His oath to your forefathers, that He brought you out with His strong hand and redeemed you from the place of slavery, from the power of Pharaoh, king of Egypt. Know then that the Lord your God is God, the steadfast God;

with those who love Him and keep His commandments He keeps covenant and faith for a thousand generations, but those who defy and reject Him He repays with destruction.... Therefore, observe conscientiously the Instruction—the laws and the rules—with which I charge you today. (Deut. 7:6–11)

Chosenness in Historical Context

This citation from Deuteronomy is interesting for a number of reasons, but in order to arrive at a better sense of its meaning we need to consider the Hebrew language of the original. The text uses the verb *bachar* (choose) two times. The literal meaning of the Hebrew in verse 6 is: "For you are a holy people to the Lord your God; the Lord God chose *you* [the *you* is emphasized in the Hebrew] for Him as a treasured people from all the peoples on the face of the earth." And in verse 9, the Hebrew literally reads, "Know then that YHWH [the four consonants that make up the name of the God of Israel], your god, is *The* God, the [truly] trustworthy god, keeping the covenant of loyalty with those who love Him and those who keep His commandments to the thousandth generation."[9]

This foundational message has two parts. First, the God of Israel is the only true god. Second, that one true God chose Israel from all the peoples of the earth to be God's own. We have seen how this sense of unique relationship is natural in the ancient Near East. In the premonotheistic period, the tribal confederation known as Israel had a unique relationship with its own tribal god, known at one time by a personal name made up of four letters. It was, of course, logical for that tribal group to be the most beloved by its own tribal deity. When that god became conceived of as the One Great God of the universe, it was instinctive for the people to retain that feeling of special relationship between deity and tribe. In fact, being the lone community that revered the only real deity, the One Great God, probably enhanced the sense of special and unique relationship.

The term *to choose* is not the only reference to the special relationship between God and Israel indicated in the Hebrew Bible. The prophet Amos refers to the relationship with the Hebrew verb *yada'*, meaning "to know intimately": "You alone have I known among all the families of the earth" (Amos 3:2). The language here is personal, with the word *mishpachot* (families) in place of the more common *'amim* (peoples).

"A people holy to the Lord ..." in verse 6 of the Deuteronomy passage above (Deut.7:6) is rendered in the Hebrew as *'am qadosh ... l'adonai*. The root meaning of *qadosh* is "to separate, put aside, or consider unique." In the religious context of the premonotheistic ancient Near East, Israel was probably no more unique in relation to its tribal god than any other ethno-religious unit was in relation to its own tribal deities. But when Israel had reached the point where it truly considered its god to be the One Great God of the universe, the relationship had indeed become unique. Given the reality of all other peoples recognizing multiple deities, the contextual environment required that Israel remain separate in order to survive under the heavy pressure toward religious assimilation.

In other words, the notion of chosenness originated simply as a natural part of old tribal religion. When Israel's concept of divinity became one of universal monotheism, it was natural to continue to feel the special relationship. After all, the God of the universe is also known in the Bible as the "God of Israel." That natural sense of chosenness also became a convenient and effective strategy to maintain a unique religious system despite the many temptations of polytheism. All religionists of the period felt that they were "chosen" by their gods. But as we will observe in more detail below, every one of the other Near Eastern tribal religions died out, leaving only the Israelites retaining the traditional sense of a "chosen" relationship with its once-tribal, now-universal God.

This does not mean that ancient Israelites necessarily felt smug about their chosenness, or even that they had a consistent definition for it. The Hebrew Bible itself expresses disagreement over the meaning and responsibility associated with chosenness. Some references relate to the election of Israel as a unique privilege and benefit that God gave freely to Abraham and his progeny:

> The Lord said to Abram, "Leave your own country, your kin, and your father's house, and go to a country that I will show you. I shall make you into a great nation; I shall bless you and make your name so great that it will be used in blessings: those who bless you, I shall bless; those who curse you, I shall curse. All the peoples on earth will wish to be blessed as you are blessed." (Gen. 12:1–3; cf. Exod. 19:1–6; Deut. 14:2)

Other biblical verses suggest that the Israelites earned their unique relationship through their merit. God said to Abraham after he proved willing to sacrifice his son in response to God's command:

> This is the word of the Lord: "By my own self I swear that because you have done this and have not withheld your son, your only son, I shall bless you abundantly and make your descendants as numerous as the stars in the sky or the grains of sand on the seashore. Your descendants will possess the cities of their enemies. All the nations on earth will wish to be blessed as your descendants are blessed, because you have been obedient to me." (Gen. 22:15–18; cf. Exod. 24:3–8)

Still other verses consider the status to be one requiring great responsibility and extraordinary behavior: "You alone I have known [intimately] among all the families of the earth; that is why I shall punish you for all your wrongdoing" (Amos 3:2). And other texts seem to render the chosenness of Israel as only a relative term, for God has chosen other peoples as well: "When that day comes Israel will rank as a third with Egypt and Assyria and be a blessing in the world. This is the blessing the Lord of Hosts will give: 'Blessed be

Egypt My people, Assyria My handiwork, and Israel My posses-
sion'" (Isa. 19:24). "'Are not you Israelites like the Cushites to
Me?' Says the Lord. 'Did I not bring Israel up from Egypt, and the
Philistines from Caphtor, the Aramaeans from Kir?'" (Amos 9:7).

Because all ethnic religions in the ancient Near East considered themselves unique on account of their special association with
their ethnic gods, the familiar human tendency toward ethnic elitism was naturally expressed through religious elitism as well.
Conquering peoples often insisted that local populations include
worship of the gods of the conquerors in local ritual. The Assyrian
king Tiglath-Pileser III (744–727 BCE), for example, had the following written about his conquest of Gaza: "As to Hanno of Gaza
who had fled before my army and run away to Egypt [I conquered]
the town of Gaza ... his personal property, his images ... [I placed
(?)] (the images of) my [... gods] and my royal image in his own
palace ... and declared (them) to be (thenceforward) the gods of
their country."[10]

When the great Persian king Cyrus (557–529 BCE) conquered
Babylon, he justified his conquest, in part, on account of the sin of
the Babylonian king Nabonidus, who refused to worship the local
Babylonian god, Marduk.

> The lord of the gods (i.e., Marduk) became terribly angry
> and [he departed from] their region.... He scanned and
> looked (through) all the countries, searching for a righteous
> ruler willing to lead them (in the annual procession). (Then)
> he pronounced the name of Cyrus, king of Anshan, declared
> him to be the ruler of all the world.... I resettled upon the
> command of Marduk, the great lord, all the gods of Sumer
> and Akkad, whom Nabonidus has brought into Babylon to
> the anger of the lord of the gods, unharmed, in their (for-
> mer) chapels, the places which make them happy. May all
> the gods whom I have resettled in their sacred cities ask
> daily (the gods) Bel and Nebo for a long life for me and may
> they recommend me.[11]

Sometimes conquering peoples merged their own gods with local gods that had parallel "job descriptions." Gods of the conquerors that were associated with certain attributes were sometimes fused with local gods having similar traits. When the Greeks conquered Egypt, for example, they simply merged their own system into the systems already in place in Egypt under the pharaohs. The Greek kings then fancied themselves as pharaohs as well, with the result that the Egyptian god Osiris, for example, was merged with the Greek god Dionysis, and the Egyptian god Thoth with the Greek god Hermes. The result was the weakening of the local religions and assimilation to a system that was closer to the religion of the conquerors.

The Greeks brought not only their gods, but also their culture. The power and popularity of Hellenic culture influenced local cultures and "hellenized" them. This resulted in the emergence of what historians call "Hellenism," a synthesis of pure Greek (Hellenic) culture with local Near Eastern cultures. Many locals learned the Greek language and integrated their traditional indigenous cultures with that of the Greeks. They were inevitably attracted to the Greek religious system as well. Because of the overwhelming and unifying power of Hellenism, local tribal nations began to lose some of the distinctiveness of their culture. Eventually, the independent integrity of the local Near Eastern religious systems would die out entirely to this assimilation, though that process would not be complete until the arrival of the Romans.

The assimilation process encouraged by the Greek and Roman conquerors was not successful, however, under the strident monotheism of Israel. By the time the Greeks had come to the area, the Israelites had become localized in a region called Judea and increasingly referred to themselves as Judeans, from which we get the term *Jew*. One of the problems that Jews faced after the Greek conquest was that they were expected, like all foreign peoples, to make offerings to the Greek gods. Because they simply and adamantly refused to do so, a compromise was eventually reached that allowed the Jews to worship in their own unique manner and make donations to their temple in Jerusalem.

When the Romans took over, they imposed their own religious system, requiring that subjugated peoples make offerings to the Roman gods, including, eventually, the figure of the Roman emperor. The traditional ethnic religions that were organized around local gods could not compete against the cultural might and attractiveness of the Romans and their gods. Because the local religions were organized around the idea that many gods existed and powered the universe, it became easy for them to make offerings to the Roman gods as well. Like the Greeks before them, the Romans unified the region culturally, and local tribal nations and religions naturally integrated with that of the conquerors. Under the Romans, many indigenous communities lost most of their unique cultural and religious identities, succumbing to the imperial system and assimilating into it. As with the Greeks, however, the monotheistic Jews could not assimilate into the Roman system. They were "grandfathered" by the Romans based on the policy of their Greek predecessors, and thus remained exempt from worshiping the Roman gods and emperors.

The Emergence of Christianity

We have noted how this period of Late Antiquity was a time of religious consolidation. The Romans had conquered many local peoples and their gods and assimilated them into the Roman system. But it was also a period of religious diffusion. The Roman system did not satisfy the religious and spiritual needs of many in the empire. As a result, new religious movements began to emerge. One category of these new religions is sometimes referred to as "mystery cults," such as Eleusinian mysteries, Mithraic mysteries (or Mithraism), and Orphic mysteries. Even the native Judeans, most of whom were steadfast in their monotheism, were profoundly affected by the powerful intellectual and cultural influence of Greece and Rome. A number of movements began to develop within the monotheist framework that was later called Judaism. Pharisees, Saducees, Essenes, and other groups emerged during this time, including movements that expected a messianic figure to lead the Jews out from under the yoke of the Roman Empire. Adherents of these various groups argued with one another over their ideas and their positions on Jewish practice, theology, and the meaning of scripture and God's expectations for Jews and humanity at large.

One of the most significant new movements to emerge out of Judean monotheism formed around the leadership of an extraordinary Jewish preacher who eventually became known as "Jesus, the messiah"—"Jesus Christ." Like the other monotheistic movements, this group refused to recognize the Roman gods or worship the emperor. We do not know exactly how and when it happened, but this group, now often referred to in scholarship as the Jesus movement, came to be recognized as distinct from the other Judean monotheistic movements. This prevented it from being grandfathered by the empire as was Judaism, which had been previously recognized by the Greeks. The Jesus movement grew quickly. It was eventually considered a threat to the empire and was brutally persecuted. Yet Christian monotheism, like the other monotheist movements, could not compromise the exclusive relationship with its singular God.

The stubbornness of the early Christians illustrates what became a phenomenon of monotheism: an absolute requirement of undivided bond between monotheists and their God. The ancient feeling of chosenness between a nation and its deity among polytheistic religions had become weakened when the local gods were so thoroughly defeated by the gods of Greece and Rome. Many local polytheists were able to make the transition to the dominant religious system, partly because of their aspiration to be accepted by the empire and eventually become Roman citizens. But the exclusive relationship between monotheists and their universal god never weakened. The One Great God was always unique, different, and greater than any and all of the national gods, even the gods of the empire. Harassment and persecution by the forces of the empire did not prove the weakening of the monotheistic God. On the contrary, monotheists believed that God would bring about divine judgment against all the empires and redemption for the chosen few who followed the truth of their faith. God may be testing the chosen ones, even sometimes through great pain and suffering, but they would never be abandoned.

One final observation must be included here: the monotheistic requirement of exclusive relationship became experienced by some believers as a social truth. That is to say, people within monotheistic communities have tended to understand their chosenness not simply as a theological relationship, but also as a social and human value. They sometimes considered their special relationship with God to indicate or even epitomize their status as inherently better, more civilized or virtuous, than others among God's human creations. Perhaps as people suffered for their exclusive loyalty to the One Great God, they came to feel that their special relationship made them inherently more godly and righteous than others. That association among some monotheists of chosenness with arrogance and self-importance would sometimes result in terrible abuse of others who were not considered part of God's chosen community.

In any event, by the emergence of Christianity, a process that began in the ancient world had reached its natural conclusion. The notion of chosenness emerged in the ancient Near East, where ethnic polytheists naturally felt a unique relationship with their national gods. It was as if each nation's god had chosen a single people for a unique, symbiotic relationship in which the people fed the god through sacrificial worship, and the god fed the people through providing fertility and protection. In the earliest period, the Israelites were like other polytheistic peoples and had their own special bond with their God of Israel. That feeling of unique attachment continued among the Israelites even as they became believers in monotheism and the old symbiosis dissolved. No longer would God need the worship of believers, but believers would always need the worshipful relationship with God. Their organic sense of being chosen by the One Great God served also as a survival mechanism for Israelite monotheism in an overwhelmingly polytheistic world. By the Roman period and the decline and eventual extinction of ethnic polytheist religions, that ancient sense of chosenness had become a trait that was deeply associated with belief in one God. It would become a defining trait of all subsequent expressions of monotheism.

3

Best Practice Models and Religious Success

New Religious Movements

New religious movements did not appear only in the Roman period. They appear in every generation, and we are witnesses to the emergence of many new religious movements in our own day. We usually call these movements sects or cults. In the academic study of religion, new religious movements became a field of interest beginning in the seventies (insiders refer to them as NRMs), and it is estimated that thousands have been born since the end of World War II. Some of those that are better known include International Society for Krishna Consciousness (or Hare Krishna, founded 1966), the Family (or Children of God, founded 1968), Aum Shinrikyo (founded 1986), Falun Gong (founded 1992), Church of Scientology (founded 1954), the Unification Church (or "Moonies," founded 1954), the Way International (founded 1942) and Wicca (founded 1951). Many well-known and well-respected religions of today were founded as new religious movements during the century before World War II, such as the Pentecostal movement, the Church of Jesus Christ of Latter-day Saints (Mormons), Jehovah's Witnesses, Bahá'í Faith, and Christian Science.

One of the questions that scholars in the field ask is why new religious movements come into existence. A definitive answer is hard to come by, since our human interest in spirituality and religion is deeply associated with the complexity of human nature and the search for meaning and a life of the spirit. Perhaps our unending spiritual drive is what was meant by the biblical notion of humanity having been created in the image of God. Certainly, our need to be true to our own inner spirit motivates many of us to think deeply about religious issues and evaluate where we fit into the religious framework that we are a part of. Some individuals seem to be open to a fresh religious call and are willing to pursue a new course.

Sometimes new religious movements emerge as factions within existing religions. These are usually called sects. They may begin as particularly active segments of the religious mainstream, or they may become inspired by a strong or charismatic leader. These groups usually remain committed to the larger institution, but occasionally they begin to see themselves as different enough from the mainstream to be considered (either by themselves or by others) as moving beyond the margins of acceptability. Under pressure from the mainstream, they may return to the fold, but that pressure may also make them feel uncomfortable enough that they seek independence. Sometimes they are pushed out. Once the faction is defined as having separated from the institution, the pressure from the mainstream often changes to hostility. If it moves far enough away from the core, it is labeled a heresy.

Sometimes a new religious movement does not emerge from within an established religious system, but from outside of it. When this occurs, it is institutionally independent and, in our day, is called a cult. *Sect, heresy,* and *cult* are all negative terms, and they indicate how the mainstream feels about them. The new movements may indeed be outrageous, but whether they are or not, mainstream reaction to them is quite consistent. The new movements are always opposed. They are threatening. They challenge the assumptions and comfort that we derive from our own religion, and they may stimulate or activate our occasional uncertainty about what we believe in. They also challenge many of the basic assumptions that we take for granted in our religions. They may also confuse our children, who are naïve and vulnerable. And, most threatening, they may be tempting enough to our children to take them away from us!

The Opposition

Establishment religion always opposes new religions. Sometimes establishment opposition to new religious movements is expressed by ignoring their existence with the hope that they will collapse on their own and disappear. And, in fact, most new religious movements do die out within a generation. But not all new religions fail, and mainstream opposition to them can become quite aggressive. Opposition to new religious movements in the Middle Ages led to violence, inquisitions, and massacres, but violence usually happens only after all other means of weakening the new movements has failed. The most common attack is by means of delegitimizing the group through public condemnation, censure, and rejection. New movements are typically identified as cults, as existing outside the realm of real spirituality. Their leaders are accused of cynically creating their own private religion in order to exploit their followers (which some have indeed done). Some are labeled as satanic or evil. All newly emerging religious movements are tagged as not being true religion.

Whether labeled as sect, heresy, or cult, if the religious movement succeeds in attracting a large enough following it becomes increasingly difficult to marginalize it. With enough followers, the new movement can withstand the pressures of the establishment to destroy it. If the movement can endure for long enough and gain a critical mass of followers, it "graduates" from being merely a movement and begins to attain the status and influence of an accepted religion.

One of the questions that students of new religious movements ask is, why do some succeed while most simply die out and disappear? In many cases, the reason for failure is quite clear. Sometimes the leader is so personally unstable that he or she is abandoned by his or her followers. In other cases, the group is so poor that it cannot sustain itself, so it falls apart and people go their own way. Sometimes bickering and poor leadership cause the movement to collapse through rancor and ill will among the members. Given the many strikes against the success of new religious movements, the more difficult question to answer is, why do some succeed?

One answer is that a successful new religion has found the true meaning of life or more closely reflects the true will of God than others, including the religious establishments. This is a common answer among adherents of the new religions themselves, but one that, needless to say, cannot be proven. Students of religious studies look at other ways to analyze the movements' success.

New Language in Thinking about Religion

Whatever the occasions of their origin, religions as we know them today are all organized and run by people. They function as institutions and, as such, they tend to behave and operate similarly to other human institutions and organizations. Some of the most insightful studies of the question of religious success use the language and theory of the market and business organization.[1] When examined as *institutions* (as opposed to divinely ordained sacred communities), religions tend to look and act in a way that is reminiscent of corporations or commercial enterprises. It is not my intent to cheapen the important spiritual and moral-ethical role of religion by comparing it morally to the cutthroat and often ethically lax operations of business. What follows is not a *moral* comparison, but rather a structural or *functional* comparison.

Religions are understood as deriving from the Infinite with the goal of realizing the will of God. Whether or not religions reflect God's true will, however, they are organized by people. Their message is delivered by people. They are represented by people, and they reach out to people. Social scientists have remarked how they tend to function *structurally*, therefore, in ways that are not so different from the ways that other human organizations function. A model that some scholars of religion have suggested to offer helpful insight into the behavior of religious institutions, therefore, is that of business organization.

For example, religions compete with one another for followers. They often promote their particular approach to God and prayer in ways that look much like some forms of advertising. Every religion offers certain benefits. All claim to help their followers live better and happier lives, and all promise personal compensation of one sort or another for belonging. Common rewards include a sense of warm community, fellowship, atonement or forgiveness of sin, spiritual fulfillment, and even everlasting life or salvation. Although the nature of religious rewards is quite different from promises of happiness or pleasure associated with purchasing a particular brand of muffin or make of dishwasher, structurally speaking, the promise of reward for consumption is identical.

In the business world, when rival companies offer different brands of the same product, such as cars or stereos, they compete with one another by trying to convince the potential consumer that *their* model will provide better quality and more advantages than that of their competition. We observe a similar kind of competition among varieties of religion. The most successful religions by most standards are those that have the largest number of adherents. Why would so many people belong if the religion were not meaningful and fulfilling? Large or growing religious movements and churches often throw around their membership numbers as a way of demonstrating that they are successful.

Those who join religious communities or participate in worship or other religious activities function as religious consumers. Every community's religious followers represent a "market share" of these consumers. When a religion controls a large market share of the religious consumer market, it becomes powerful and has a corresponding influence on society as a whole. Because a generally accepted marker of success is in the numbers, those with the greater numbers are considered most successful.

In successful religion, as in successful business, the best models tend to be emulated. In modern business this is a conscious and carefully calculated process. In religion, it is likely to be less calculated, but, as in business, a successful religion needs to control a certain share of the consumer market to avoid going "bankrupt." No religion can survive without the aid of a minimal amount of supporters' energy, commitment, personal abilities, and material resources.

To extend this business model, new religious movements can be likened to new consumer products that become available to consumers. They tend to function like a new company with its own, unique product or brand on the "religious market." In order to succeed in gaining the necessary market share of support to survive, new religious movements must demonstrate to the pool of potential consumers that they are authentic and that they have something to offer that will meet consumers' religious needs. To use more religious language, new religious movements must convince an adequate number of potential believers that they are authoritative and that they truly represent the divine will. This is public legitimatizing. It is similar to a business program of branding that establishes a sense of confidence and trust among consumers.

One way that new religions demonstrate their religious legitimacy is by representing themselves in ways that are easily recognized as authentic by potential joiners. Successful new religions do this intuitively by adopting familiar religious symbols. To take one simple and common example, new Christian religious movements always use some form of the cross as a sign that they are an authentic form of Christianity. Most other symbols of authentic religion, such as prophecy, revelation, covenant, and scripture, are not as physical, but they are no less important foundations upon which successful religion is based. We will observe below how the notion of covenant appears in the earliest literary layers of Judaism,

Christianity, and Islam as a symbol of authenticity. Leaders of new religions are usually considered by their followers to be prophets who speak in the name of God.

Successful new religious movements manage to incorporate authenticating symbols of established religions in their own representational systems. We must keep in mind that images, symbols, belief concepts, and rituals form the building blocks of religion. They are not necessarily exclusive to any one system. It is the unique *form* or style of these and their particular combinations that make for the many different expressions of religion.

One classic example of the use and reuse of previous religious symbols can be found in the emergence of ancient Israelite monotheism. For example, many Israelite customs, traditions, rituals, and conventions can be found among contemporary and more ancient neighboring religions in the ancient Near East. We have learned from the science of archaeology that the altars in ancient Israel looked like Canaanite altars. The layout of the Tabernacle and Temple look very similar to the layout of other holy structures found in ancient sites in the region. The Bible attests that there were non-Israelite priests and non-Israelite prophets (Exod. 3:1; Numbers 22). Even religious poems with uncanny linguistic and literary parallels to biblical psalms have been discovered in the libraries of ancient civilizations unearthed in archaeological digs.[2] But the language of those poems reveres other gods. What made Israelite psalms unique was the extraordinary way that they used well-known idioms and expressions in their praise and worship of the One Great God. Different religions share many of the same generic symbols and institutions. It is the unique way in which these symbols and institutions are conveyed and interpreted that provides the special nature of each religion.

Keep in mind that Israelite religion was considered ancient when it was encountered by the early Greeks in the fourth century BCE. It became the only religious survivor from the ancient Near East. The earliest Greek writers on the Jews, such as Theophrastus, Megasthenes, and Clearchus of Soli, all of whom lived in the fourth to third centuries BCE, gave Israel their highest compliment, for they considered Israel to be a nation of philosophers.[3] As a most ancient expression of God's communication to humanity, it was natural for Israel's religion to be emulated, whether consciously or not, by new religious movements in formation under the Romans and after. Those that were most successful managed to integrate some of the most powerful symbols, images, and motifs from the religion of biblical Israel. As we have learned above, one of the most central motifs of ancient Israel was chosenness.

The religion of Israel is the mother of monotheism. It was natural, therefore, that it became the definitive model for articulating the relationship with the One Great God. One classic marker of that relationship is God's revelation and its record in scripture. God's revelation of scripture is exceedingly rare, and it is always local. It may be intended for a universal audience, but it is always given to a discrete community, and it marks that community as special, unique—and limited. The extraordinary rarity of scriptural revelation and the limited nature of its reception within a distinct human community are characterized and symbolized in monotheism by the notion of chosenness. Chosenness was a natural and appealing motif to be absorbed by new religious movements because it epitomizes the unique and exclusive relationship between God and humanity. In a world of competing religions, being the one community *truly* chosen by God conveys a clear message to potential joiners who seek a meaningful religious community and a path to the Divine.

Chosenness was emblematic of Israelite religion because of its origin among ancient Near Eastern polytheisms. When the religion of Israel became the first and thus most famous expression of monotheism, it was natural for chosenness to become emblematic of new forms of monotheism as well, those trying to compete in the religious market. So when we examine the successful monotheistic religious movements that emerged out of the crucible of the ancient Near East, we cannot help but notice that they all incorporate this one foundational aspect of ancient Israelite religion. A number of other common motifs are also found among them. But chosenness, associated with scriptural revelation and authenticated by it, is at the core and incorporated by them all.

The Counterattack

Students of new religious movements have articulated something that we already know intuitively from our own experience: that both the leaders and the rank-and-file of establishment religions do not care for new religions—to say the least. Religious leaders and functionaries preach against them. They dispute with them. They claim that new religions make metaphysical promises that cannot be fulfilled. They often shame leaders of new religions and argue that they manipulate innocent people to believe in them only in order to benefit themselves. The bottom line of their argument is that new religious movements are not authoritative representations of the divine will. They are not authentic, not "true religion."

These very positions were articulated by representatives of establishment religions in reference to the Jesus movement as it emerged in Late Antiquity. They were also articulated in reference to emerging Islam. Christianity and Islam are the two most successful religions in human history, based on their share of religious consumers, and they have long since behaved like established religions. But they were once new religious movements themselves, and they suffered, as all new religious movements do, from the attacks of the establishment.

The New Testament repeatedly complains about the attitudes of the establishment that seemed so intent on destroying the new Jesus movement. Jews or Pharisees are often identified as trying to discredit Jesus and harassing his followers (Matt. 22:15–30; Mark 7:1–5, 12:13–25; Acts 5:17, 6:8–15, 8:3, 9:1–2; Gal. 4:29, 5:11; 2 Cor. 11:21–24). Romans were also opposed to the new movement and its supporters and acted forcibly against them (Acts 16:19–24; 2 Cor. 11:26). Many parts of the New Testament complain about the general persecution that Jesus and his supporters suffered (Romans 8:35; 1 Cor. 4:11–13; 2 Thess. 1:5; Heb. 10:32; 1 Pet. 4:16).

The Qur'an likewise complains about the attitudes of the establishment religions of its own day to the newly emerging movement of Islam. The major threat to Islam came from Arab polytheists, who are depicted repeatedly as trying to destroy the young movement (2:217, 3:195, 9:107, 16:110, 22:40, 41:26). Jews and Christians are sometimes lumped together as "People of the Book" in the Qur'an, and they are portrayed as consistently opposing and disparaging the Muslim movement as well (2:74–75, 2:100–101, 2:109, 3:69–72, 4:153, 5:57–59, 4:146–147).

Most new religious movements are not able to sustain themselves in the face of attacks by establishment opposition, but some are able to fight back. As the weaker party in the relationship, they are not in a position to fight physically, and often they are not even able defend themselves against physical attack. But the successful movements fight back nevertheless, and they do so through argument. They counter the accusations of the opposition and often engage in a literary counterattack. The purpose of the rhetorical thrust and parry seems not to disable the opponent so much as to provide encouragement to the beleaguered followers who suffer abuse from the establishment. Counterattack provides moral support for those who need it most.

Scripture and Polemic

You can observe this kind of argument and literary counterattack within the scriptures of Judaism, Christianity, and Islam. Passionate, urgent, and aggressive argument is called *polemic*, and polemic is deeply embedded in monotheist scripture. In fact, because the three scriptures represent the earliest record we have for the period during which the three great monotheistic religions emerged, they contain within them valuable information about the tensions, resentment, and conflict that surround their origins.

Scriptures are collections of literary materials that teach about God and tell the epic tales of the religion and its founders. They also faithfully reflect the mood and attitude of the early community of believers in the earliest stages of their emergence into history. Given the hostile environments in which new religions inevitably arise, it is not surprising to observe that scriptures articulate anger and even rage directed against the establishments that were trying to bring about the demise of the religion that they represent. Scriptures inevitably attack what is articulated as the "hypocrisy" of those representing the establishment religions that attack them (Ps. 115:1–11; Matt. 23:13–33; Qur'an 2:40–44). Some of these scriptural counterattacks are quite severe.

Based on what we now know of the difficulties encountered by new religious movements, it is not be surprising to find anti-Jewish rhetoric in the New Testament or anti-Jewish and anti-Christian rhetoric in the Qur'an. The Hebrew Bible also contains plenty of angry rhetoric directed against the Canaanite religious establishment of its own day. The New Testament is rightly condemned today for its sometimes nasty portrayals of Jews, and the Qur'an is properly criticized for its sometimes nasty portrayals of Jews and Christians. Negative and malicious portrayals of others always need to be condemned, even (or *especially*) when they occur in sacred text. We tend to pay more attention to the negative portrayals of Jews and Christians in the New Testament and the Qur'an because Jews and Christians exist today to complain about them. There are no Canaanites today to complain about their nasty image in the Hebrew Bible! All of this scriptural antagonism reflects the difficult experience of those early believers among the few emerging religions that survived.

As we work through the scenario of the birth of new religion, we need to keep one thing in mind. Persecuted new religious movements that succeed and are able to claim a healthy market share of supporters, along with the power that comes with it, eventually become *establishment* religions. When that happens, they, in turn, denigrate and attempt to delegitimate new religious movements that threaten *them*.

Mimesis, Intertextuality, and Authenticity

The term *mimesis* comes from the Greek and is an elegant English word used in the art world to describe how art can imitate life or nature (the word *mime* comes from the same root, as does the word *mimic*). In literature, mimesis is a term that describes the rhetorical use of something that has already been said. Religions are highly mimetic because they naturally use language and symbols and notions that have already been established by earlier religions, but they use them or understand them in distinctive ways that distinguish their own unique identity.

Intertextuality is a word that relates to the relationship between texts. There is an intertextual relationship, for example, between the biblical Flood story and the ancient Babylonian Epic of Gilgamesh, in which the gods cause a flood that destroys all humankind except for one man (whose name is not Noah, but Utnapishtum). Scriptures are highly intertextual because literary motifs and symbols and even names appear across and between them.

Religions are both highly mimetic and intertextual. They share many of the same symbols and themes, and that sharing occurs most often textually. We have noted above, for example, how the symbolic power of the cross is found as a legitimating motif in new Christian movements. The sharing of symbols and themes occurs freely across religious boundaries as well, and the most basic and powerful textual source of religious mimesis is scripture. We have already observed that common themes such as prophecy and revelation are foundations upon which new religions become based, and how the notion of covenant appears in the earliest literary layers of Judaism, Christianity, and Islam as a symbol of authenticity. These themes demonstrate to potential followers that the scripture, and therefore the religious movement, are genuine and legitimate.

But authenticating symbols and themes are successful exactly for the reason that they are deeply associated with the known, establishment religions. If a new religious movement incorporates too much of the establishment within it, it loses its standing as an alternative to the status quo. On the other hand, being too far out proves its own illegitimacy. Success means maintaining a balance between likeness and uniqueness.

For the new religion, this balance between likeness and uniqueness causes a certain level of anxiety. It is risky to take on the very aspects of an "other" that desires to cause your demise! At a certain conscious or unconscious level, the new religion is working to replace establishment religions. This is one of the reasons for the clear polemics in scripture associated with chosenness. Polemics are arguments and disputes that are used to support one side's own position while discrediting the position of the opposition. Scriptures contain a great deal of polemics because they are making a case for the truth and validity of the new religion that they represent. This is all happening under the pressure that is leveled against it by the establishment religions that are trying to discredit it.

Text and Subtext

Literary scholars teach that every text has its subtext(s). A subtext is an unnamed issue or passage from something written or spoken that the text is responding to. A subtext may even be a work of art or artistic style to which an artist is responding. Often the reference is indirect, such as when a comedian makes a joke out of a statement made by a political figure without referring directly to the politician or what he or she said. The politician's statement (or even the manner in which he or she makes it) is the unspoken subtext to which the comedian is responding.

In the case of scriptural polemic, a subtext may be the arguments or the aggression of the religious competition to which the scripture is responding. We do not have a lot of written material that is contemporary with the Hebrew Bible, so we cannot always be confident about specific subtexts to which it may be responding. But if you read through the biblical chosenness texts, you will note how powerful the image of chosenness is, and how it is used to separate Israelite believers from the opposition nonbelievers who seem to have been all around them: "And you shall be holy to Me, for I the Lord am holy, and I have set you apart from other peoples to be Mine" (Lev. 20:26); "Now then, if you will obey Me conscientiously and keep My covenant, you shall be My treasured possession among all the peoples" (Exod. 18:5–6); "I will maintain My covenant between Me and you, and your offspring to come, as an everlasting covenant throughout the ages" (Gen. 17:7).

Note how exclusive the language is, and how harsh: "I will bless those who bless you and curse him that curses you" (Gen. 12:3), "[The Lord your God] instantly requites with destruction those [Israelites] who reject Him" (Deut. 7:10–11).

This language is belligerent and polemical. It is challenging and threatens opponents or potential opponents, in this case unnamed. It supplies one side of an argument. We don't hear the other side, but it is clear that it is directed against an unidentified "other" who is not depicted as loyal to the one great and zealous God. Sometimes that "other" seems to represent those within the community who are unfaithful. More often, it represents the adherents of other religions. The immoral nature of other religions and the corrupt communities that practice them is a regular subtext to the polemics of the Hebrew Bible. This can reasonably be presumed from the negative references, and some of those negative references are indeed specific: "For all those abhorrent [religiously defined] things were done by the people who were in the land before you, and the land became defiled. So let not the land vomit you out … as it vomited out the nation that came before you" (Lev. 18:27–28).

We must keep in mind that the term for "nation" in this as in many such verses, *goy,* refers to a religious nation, since religion and nation were so closely associated in the ancient Near East. No ancient Near Eastern canon of scripture that predates the Hebrew Bible has yet been uncovered, though religious poetry, such as poems to neighboring gods, have been discovered in archaeological digs. The general subtext in the case of the Hebrew Bible polemic is the religious practices and opposition of Israel's neighbors. There is no direct subtext to the claim of exclusive chosenness in the Hebrew Bible. We do have scriptural subtexts for chosenness polemics in the New Testament, however, and these are found in the Hebrew Bible. We also have subtexts for Qur'anic chosenness polemics. They occur in both the Hebrew Bible and the New Testament.

The New Testament claims a new chosenness applied to those who have chosen to follow Jesus. The subtext is the chosen status of Israel, which is replaced in the New Testament with the chosen status of those, whether Jew or Gentile, who believe in the messiahship of Jesus. In a kind of irony, it is the Hebrew biblical claim to the elite chosen status of Israel that serves to authenticate the new claim for divine election among Christians. Of course, an argument must make that case, and we find it appearing in various forms in the New Testament. The following example is from 1 Peter:

> So for you who have faith it has great worth; but for those who have no faith "the stone which the builders rejected has become the corner-stone," and also "a stone to trip over, a rock to stumble against." They trip because they refuse to believe the word; this is the fate appointed for them. But you are a chosen race, a royal priesthood, a dedicated nation, a people claimed by God for His own, to proclaim the glorious deeds of Him who has called you out of darkness into His marvelous light. Once you were not a people at all; but now you are God's people. Once you were outside His mercy; but now you are outside no longer. (2:7–10)

A literary subtext for this passage is Psalm 118:22–23: "The stone that the builders rejected has become the chief cornerstone. This is the Lord's doing; it is marvelous in our sight." The Psalm text is a consolation to Israel, which is represented as the rejected stone that has (or more likely, will soon) become the cornerstone.

But the New Testament refers to the rejected stone in two ways. First, it represents the followers of Jesus who were rejected by most Jews but will soon become the cornerstone of God's new dispensation. And second, it represents the new dispensation that the Jews trip over and stumble against because they cannot accept it. The metaphor serves as moral support for a new religious community, rejected by establishment religionists, that actually takes on the very status that the establishment claimed for itself. A second subtext for this passage is the notion articulated by a number of biblical verses that the covenant between God and Israel is conditional on Israel keeping the covenant, as in Exodus 19:5–6: "Now then, if you will obey Me conscientiously and keep My covenant, you shall be My treasured possession among all the peoples. Indeed, all the earth is Mine, but you shall be to Me a kingdom of priests and a holy nation." This notion is taken to mean in the Peter text that keeping the divine covenant means accepting and believing the new revelation and new covenant that God has made through Jesus. The Gentile believers were outside the covenant of biblical Israel, but by accepting Jesus they are outside no longer. According to this passage (along with others that provide additional support) both Jews and Gentiles may be a part of the new covenant, but that new covenant is based on faith—in the saving power of Jesus—rather than law (Eph. 2:8), and it proves the annulment of the old covenant.

> In fact, the ministry which has fallen to Jesus is as far superior to theirs as are the covenant he mediates and the promises upon which it is legally secured. Had the first covenant been faultless, there would have been no need to look for a second in its place. But God, finding fault with them, says, "The days are coming, says the Lord, when I will conclude a new covenant … [Jeremiah 31:30]." By speaking of a new covenant, he has pronounced the first one old; and anything that is growing old and aging will shortly disappear. (Heb. 8:6–13)

This is a classic example of a new religion taking on authenticating motifs of an established religion, in this case, the symbolic institution of covenant. The very motif that was claimed to authenticate the established religion is used to reject it and legitimize the new in its place.

The Qur'an engages in a similar polemic by making the case that both Jews and Christians have forfeited their exclusive claims to being God's chosen. The subtexts in this passage are more general than in the New Testament passage just cited, but the rejection of earlier claims is based on images and institutions (such as covenant) that appear frequently in both the Hebrew Bible and the New Testament.

> God made a covenant with the Children of Israel, and We sent them twelve chiefs. God said: I am with you. If you engage in prayers, contribute the required charity, believe in My messengers and honor them, and support the religion, I will absolve you from your evil deeds and cause you to enter Gardens through which rivers flow, so whoever of you disbelieves after that has strayed from the right way. And because of their breaking their covenant We have cursed them and made their hearts hard. They change the words from their places and forgot part of what they were reminded [through revelation]. You will continue to discover the treacherous among them except for a few, but forgive them and pardon, for God loves the good. And those who say: "We are Christians," We made their covenant but they forgot a part of what they were reminded [through revelation]. So We incited enmity and hatred between them until the Day of Resurrection, when God will tell them what they have done. (5:12–14)

We have considered thus far how Christianity and Islam began as new religious movements that were strongly opposed by the religious establishments of their day, but nevertheless met with success. They succeeded in gaining the necessary share of supporters to survive the natural opposition of establishment religions and other threatened establishment powers. They were so successful, in fact, they quickly thrived and grew into the two most powerful religious movements in human history. Many factors contributed to their extraordinary success, but certainly their ability to demonstrate their legitimacy early on was critical. Each made the case that it represented a new dispensation that was better than the religious options available, and each claimed the banner that had been waived by the biblical monotheism of Israel. But what of that early monotheism that was represented by biblical Israel? What ever happened to it?

The short answer is that biblical monotheism died long ago. The religion of the Bible did not long survive the destruction of the Jerusalem Temple. In phenomenological terms, one could justifiably refer to both Christianity and Islam as heirs and successors to biblical religion. In fact, however, biblical religion did not produce only two heirs. It produced a third heir as well: rabbinic Judaism.

The "New Religion" of Judaism

At about the same time that a new revelation emerged, according to Christians, in the person of Jesus, another repository of revelation was emerging according to Jews who did not accept the messiahship and divinity of Jesus. That is the Talmud, also called the Oral Torah, to be distinguished by Jews from the Written Torah of the Hebrew Bible. Contrary to some uninformed assumptions, the religion of Israel did not remain static after the emergence of Christianity. It continued to evolve with the destruction of the Jerusalem Temple and the end of sacrifice and other rituals and structures of biblical religion. Just as Christianity is not the same religion as that of biblical Israel, rabbinic Judaism—the Judaism exemplified by the Rabbis of the Talmud and that which is practiced in one form or another by virtually all Jews today—is also not the same as the religion of biblical Israel. Different worship (the use of synagogues instead of the Temple, no more sacrifices, different liturgy), different theologies, different behavioral obligations, and different expectations of the End of Days mark only some of the many significant distinctions; and of course, although unadvertised, an additional scripture in the Oral, as opposed to Written, Torah of rabbinic Judaism. Such differences are the stuff that makes for a different religion.

The reason that this has not attracted more attention is that the Jews representing rabbinic Judaism in Late Antiquity (roughly 100–600 CE) did not intend to make an obvious break with the ancient religious system as did those who accepted the saving power of Jesus as Messiah. For the new Christians, breaking away from the establishment religions was essential, despite the need to retain a level of continuity for reasons that we have considered above. For the Jews, it was *continuity* that was essential for maintaining its claim of authenticity, so the scriptural nature of the Talmud emerged gradually and only became a doctrinal expectation for most Jews in the eighth century. But the Talmud functions similarly to the New Testament, as a lens through which the Hebrew Bible is read. That is to say, similar to the way in which Christians read the Old Testament through the interpretive lens of the New Testament, Jews read the Hebrew Bible through the interpretive lens of the Talmud.

Even among Protestant Christian denominations that claim to go directly to scripture without the interference of the magisterium of the "One Holy Catholic Apostolic Church," the Old Testament cannot be read meaningfully without looking at it through the lens of the New. So, too, in Jewish tradition, among all but a tiny group known as Kara'ites, the Hebrew Bible is read through the eyes of rabbinic literature, which for purposes of discussion here can be referred to as the Talmud.[4] It is certainly true that the *way* in which it is read varies greatly among Jewish communities (just as the way in which the Bible is read varies among Christian communities), but it is the broad range of Talmudic interpretation that concretizes the meanings of the Bible for Jews. The emergence of tradition that resulted in the development of the Talmud pushes the boundaries between revelation and interpretation even further than the New Testament does. Nevertheless, its recognition in Judaism as Oral Torah renders it scripture.[5]

In sum, then, the old religion of Israel began as a simple form of polytheism that changed and developed into the first successful form of monotheism. This is the religion of the Hebrew Bible, and it is both the "mother of monotheisms" and the progenitor of scriptural religions. There *is* no more biblical religion outside the text of the Hebrew Bible. Nobody practices it. The chosenness that is so central and deliberate in the Hebrew Bible is an institution and symbolic paradigm that has been absorbed in one way or another by all of its surviving monotheistic progeny.

How has rabbinic Judaism understood chosenness? After all, anyone who observes history might conclude that Israel has lost its chosen status. Just look at the size of the Jewish population throughout the world (about 15 million) in relation to the size of the Muslim (about 1.3 billion) and Christian (about 2.1 billion) populations. In point of fact, the experience of permanent exile and inferior social and political status in relation to Christians and Muslims forced a high level of complexity and ambivalence within Jewish thinking about chosenness. On the one hand, because of the great stress on continuity, rabbinic Judaism buys into the chosenness of Israel expressed in the Hebrew Bible and claims it. It then applies the chosen status of biblical Israel to the continuation of Israel among the Jews of the world. On the other hand, the Talmud and rabbinic literature express a certain discomfort with this sense of essential superiority. One repeated sentiment is that God did not choose Israel because of its inherent superiority, but rather because there were no other takers:

> Is it not written: "The Lord came from Sinai and rose from Seir unto them, He shined forth from Mount Paran" (Deut. 32:2)? And it is also written: "God comes from Teman" (Hab. 3:3)? What did God seek in Seir and what did God

seek in Paran? Rabbi Yonahan said: This teaches us that the Holy One offered the Torah to every nation and every tongue, but none accepted it, until God came to Israel, who accepted it. (Talmud, Avodah Zarah 2b)

In an alternative tradition, God eventually had to force one people to accept the difficult life of Torah commandments, and that people ended up being Israel:

Moses led the people out of the camp toward God, and they took their places *at the foot of* [in the Hebrew, it can also mean "underneath"] the mountain (Exod.19:17). Rav Avdimi bar Hama bar Hasa said: "This teaches that the Holy One turned the mountain over above them like an [over-turned] cask and said to them: 'If you accept the Torah, good. But if not, this shall be your grave!'" (Talmud, Shabbat 88a)

In a third, Abraham and his progeny were "chosen" by the angels, but only by the casting of lots, not because Israel was inherently better than any other nation:

Rabbi Shimon said: The Holy One called to the seventy angels who surround the throne of glory and said to them: Come, let us descend and confuse the seventy nations and the seventy languages. From where [do we know] that the Holy One spoke [thus] to them? Because it says, "Let us go down" (Gen. 11:7). "I will go down" is not written, but "Let *us* go down." They [the angels] cast lots among them, as it says, "When the Most High gave the nations their inheritance, when [God] divided humanity" (Deut. 32:8). The lot of the Holy One fell upon Abraham and his descendants, as it says, "For the Lord's portion is His people, Jacob is the lot of his inheritance" (Deut. 32:9). (Pirqey Rabbi Eliezer 24)

Not all rabbinic expressions of chosenness are so modest, however. The Talmud emerged as an authoritative literature during and after the rise of Christianity, so it was able to offer counter-arguments to Christian claims of having acquired the old Israelite status of chosenness. In the statement that follows, God is depicted as knowing the future decline of the Jews under the Romans, but nevertheless affirms that the eternal chosen status of the Jews was established even before creation:

> Rabbi Eliezer HaModa'i said [narrating in the voice of God] … "Was [Israel] not already designated by Me even before the six days of creation?" As it is said, "If these laws [of Creation] should ever be annulled by Me—declares the Lord—only then would the offspring of Israel cease to be a nation before Me forever" (Jer. 31:35). (Mekhilta de Rabbi Yishmael, Beshalach 3)

We have observed from the texts cited above that after the notion of chosenness was established through ancient Israelite religion and had become a respected marker of authentic monotheism, Jews, Christians, and Muslims jockeyed for relative status by making claims to chosenness for themselves. These expressions of chosenness, however, are not alike. Each one expresses the claim through the unique nature of the religious system that it represents, and their representations have been profoundly influenced by the historical contexts in which each system emerged. We will soon examine how each religious civilization behaved toward nonbelievers in ways that were influenced by their particular notion of election, but in order to get there we need to consider how the sense of chosenness differs among them.

4

Chosenness and Covenant in the New Testament

The New Testament represents God's message to the world as conveyed by the acts and words of Jesus. No ordinary prophet, Jesus was God incarnate, so his words and deeds—and the accompanying explanations of their meaning recorded in scripture—are no less than the direct message of God. The original texts of the New Testament were written in Greek and date from about 45 CE to about 145 CE, but the decision as to which of these should be included in the canon of official scripture took centuries to become finalized. This was a process that reflected the particulars of the historical context in which it occurred. That context was the Near East of Late Antiquity.

Christianity and the Religious Context of Roman Palestine

The late antique Near East was quite different from the ancient Near East discussed in the previous chapters. Divided between the two great empires of Persia and Rome, religion was much less tribal, more universal both in physical range and worldview. The national religion of Persia was a form of Zoroastrianism, while the national religion of Rome was a kind of paganism that had been

profoundly influenced by Greek and Roman pantheism, Greek philosophy, Roman administrative and political interests, and ideas and
notions that had been current in the old indigenous Near Eastern
religions. As noted earlier, the Jesus movement emerged in an environment in which established religions were under strain. The old
Roman system was not meeting the spiritual and religious needs of
many Greco-Romans. Similarly, the old biblical system, centered
around the Jerusalem Temple, which had been weakened by the loss
of Judean political independence, was profoundly challenged by the
new ideas represented by Greece and Rome, and somewhat less so
by Persian religion and culture. By the year of Jesus's birth, the religion of biblical Israel had lost much of its luster.

New religious movements were springing up from within the
pagan and monotheistic religious worlds, and their leaders naturally competed for influence and support. In the cosmopolitan culture of Roman Judea, they discussed and argued with one another
about the tenets and assumptions of their faith. One of these movements coalesced around the person of Jesus. It is now quite clear
that Jesus lived his life as a Jew, and his followers were also Jews.
But exactly what *kind* of Jews Jesus and his community represented
is not at all clear. Just as the ancient religion of Israel was not
monolithic (recall the many religious customs and practices that
were uprooted by Josiah's reforms mentioned in 2 Kings 23), neither was the Judaism at the time of Jesus monolithic. Various
movements that are identified as sometimes political and sometimes religious—remember the intimate connection between religion and peoplehood or polity in the Near East—were battling one
another in words and deeds over dominance over the Jews of
Judea.

These were battles about Jewish identity and meaning in a
world in which so many of the old assumptions could no longer be
certain. Where was God in a world of Roman oppression and weak
Jewish leadership? Uncertainty about the future of Israel was
endemic. Changes were weakening the unity of the community and
the meaning and efficacy of Temple ritual. The resulting insecurity

and malaise were shaking the very foundations of Judaism. Many considered an endtime immanent, the possibility of an apocalypse that would entirely change the world order.

A number of popular movements emerged during this period that intended to bring the Judean community back on track. These included popular prophetic movements and others that we now refer to as messianic movements—groups that expected a political or military redeemer, a descendant of King David, to restore the Davidic monarchy of old. Under Roman occupation some groups seem to have expected the arrival of a more miraculous figure who would redeem Israel both physically and spiritually, and they attracted followings during Jesus's lifetime.[1] Jesus's messianic identity was thus tied intimately to his religious and political context. He preached and ministered in the Galilee, a region in what is today northern Israel, and his association with miracles and compassionate, charismatic leadership gained him disciples and followers.

Jesus was known as a healer who would make things right again. He cast out demons (Mark 1:32–34) and even brought the dead back to life (Matt. 9:18–26), an act that certainly awed his witnesses but was not considered unbelievable (Elijah had done the same in 1 Kings 17:17–24). He argued with his Jewish compatriots over the meaning of God's will, and like many other Jews, he reminded all who would listen of the immanent coming of God's kingdom (Mark 1:14–15).

Jesus lived at a time and in a place of political and religious instability, a historical period rife with intense argument and polemic. All four Gospels depict Jesus in repeated controversy with Jews, especially scribes and Pharisees, who are portrayed as representing a rigid Jewish establishment perspective that lacked real spirituality (Matt. 23, Mark 12, Luke 20, John 7). The issues around which Jesus and other Jewish leaders of his time preached and argued with their fellows were never resolved during his lifetime. The controversy and polemic that would become so emblematic of the relationship between the religions of Christianity and Judaism thus actually began as internal arguments among Jews.

Jesus had many enemies, both Roman and Jewish, and they are depicted in New Testament sources as conspiring to bring about his demise and death. He was humiliated, physically abused, and then crucified. His ignominious end was a great shock for his followers, who were shattered by the brutal dashing of their highest hopes. But the story did not end with Jesus's humiliation. What occurred next was the extraordinary event of the resurrection, not witnessed but nevertheless proven to many, first tentatively by an empty tomb, and then by Jesus's personal appearance before several of his followers (Matthew 28, Luke 24). And it was the resurrection that proved his redemptive, messianic status, confirmed by Jesus himself, who appeared unrecognized before two of his followers and said, "'Was not the Messiah bound to suffer in this way before entering upon his glory?' Then, starting from Moses and all the prophets, he explained to them in the whole of scripture the things that referred to himself" (Luke 24:26–27).

Eventually, and in common with what academics refer to as a process of sect formation and then transition from sect to new religion, the Jesus movement evolved into a separate religious institution. It came to be recognized both by its own adherents and by those outside the community as a discrete faith called Christianity, the religion of Christ or "the anointed one" (in Greek, *Christos*). As this happened, some of the earlier internal Jewish arguments were recast as arguments among believers representing separate faith communities. Because the Gospels were not canonized until at least the third and perhaps even the fourth century, this transition from internal Jewish argument to Jewish-Christian polemic is reflected even in the texts of scripture. And the followers of Jesus did indeed become a separate faith community that stood outside the broadest margins of the movements that we identify as the Jewish movements of Late Antiquity.

The process of separation and differentiation is popularly referred to in academic discourse as the "parting of the ways." It is complex, and scholars are not in agreement over many of its details. But it is clear that when the two communities recognized their distinct identities as unique and mutually exclusive, the polemic that was built up around the old Near Eastern notion of chosenness reached a high level of intensity.

One of the signature differences between the separating faith communities was their notion of covenantal relationship with God. In the Jewish system, which retained the biblical notion of religious peoplehood as it evolved into Judaism, covenantal membership derived from birth of a Jewish mother or formal religious study and conversion. It required circumcision, acknowledgment of the divine origin and eternal validity of Torah, and personal loyalty to the required ritual, civic, and moral-ethical behaviors set down in the Torah and its interpretation. Although Gentiles could be rewarded by God on this earth and even in the world to come, they could not be a part of God's covenanted people without these.

Among Christians, on the other hand, after passing through the early period when virtually all followers of Jesus were Jews of one form or another, the overwhelming majority of believers were Gentiles, and circumcision was no longer a requirement for covenant membership. Neither was obedience to what came to be considered by Christians to be an outmoded system of law that had been superseded by God's grace. Gentiles became part of God's new covenant through personal faith in the saving power of Jesus as Christ-Messiah. Not only were they welcomed into the new covenantal community, but they also became the exclusive holders of a new covenantal relationship in Christ that excluded all Jews who either would not or could not accept his transcendent status.

This position was of course strongly opposed by the Jewish establishment. The Jews were well-established monotheists who were generally deeply respected in Greco-Roman society, even if rather resented. The burden was on the new Christian community to authenticate the new movement in terms that would demonstrate the truth of its claims. Those who followed Jesus naturally found support for the truth of his mission in the world around them, and like the Jesus of Luke 24:27 who explained to his disciples how references in "the whole of scripture"—meaning the

Hebrew Bible—pointed to his messiahship, they looked to the Hebrew Bible for support as well. Those who believed in Jesus saw clear scriptural proofs and prophecies of his birth, mission, death, and resurrection. They also saw that the chosen, covenantal relationship between God and Abraham depicted in scripture was actually a proof of the new chosen status of those who had faith in Christ.

Chosen through Faith

Romans 4 is devoted to making sense of the mystery of God having chosen Abraham. "What does scripture say? 'Abraham put his faith in God, and that faith was counted to him as righteousness'" (4:3). Abraham was chosen by God for his faith rather than for his obedience, for his relationship with God began even before he was asked to prove his obedience to God through circumcision and the establishment of the covenant (4:4–12). "It was not through law that Abraham and his descendants were given the promise that the world should be their inheritance but through righteousness that came from faith" (4:13). The following few verses make the case that obedience to the law, which was the cornerstone of emerging rabbinic Judaism, was not the real purpose of God's chosen relationship with Abraham. Abraham's having been chosen by God was, rather, on account of his faith, and that faith includes, by extension, faith in resurrection and salvation through Jesus.

> If the heirs are those who hold by the law, then faith becomes pointless and the promise goes for nothing.... The promise was made on the ground of faith in order that it might be a matter of sheer grace, and that it might be valid for all Abraham's descendants, not only for those who hold by the law, but also for those who have Abraham's faith, for he is father of us all.... His faith did not weaken.... And that is why Abraham's faith was "counted to him as righteousness." The words, "counted to him" were meant to apply not only

to Abraham but to us; our faith too is to be "counted," the faith in the God who raised Jesus our Lord from the dead; for he was given up to death for our misdeeds, and raised to life for our justification. (Rom. 4:14–25)

The letter of James argues the same point and concludes by connecting God's special designation of Abraham as "loving friend" with Abraham's absolute faith. "Was it not by his action, in offering his son Isaac upon the altar, that our father Abraham was justified? Surely you can see faith was at work in his actions, and by these actions his faith was perfected? Here was fulfillment of the words of scripture: 'Abraham put his faith in God, and that faith was counted to him as righteousness,' and he was called 'God's friend'" (James 2:21–23).

As important as Abraham is to Christianity, however, the new symbol of God's most intimate relationship with humanity is Jesus. Jesus represents the quintessence of intimacy, and God's love for Jesus, God's own son, becomes transferred through Jesus's sacrifice to all those who would have faith in him. At one level, then, the chosen is Jesus, described in the New Testament as the divinely chosen descendent of David identified as the Messiah:

Do not be afraid, Mary, for you have found favor with God. And behold, you will conceive in your womb and bear a son, and you shall call his name Jesus. He will be great, and will be called the Son of the Most High; and the Lord God will give to him the throne of his father David, and he will reign over the house of Jacob forever; and of his kingdom there will be no end. (Luke 1:30–33)

The subtext for this passage is 2 Samuel 7:12–13, when God tells David, "When your days are fulfilled and you lie down with your fathers, I will raise up your offspring after you, one of your own issue, and I will establish his kingship. He shall build a house for My name, and I will establish his royal throne forever. I will be

a father to him, and he shall be a son to Me.... Your house and your
kingship shall ever be secure before you; your throne shall be established forever."

In a later passage in the same Gospel, the actual words used by
God to confirm Jesus's authoritative status includes the idiom of chosenness: "There came a cloud which cast its shadow over them; they
were afraid as they entered the cloud, and from it a voice spoke: 'This
is My son, My Chosen; listen to him'" (Luke 9:35). Other passages
also single out Jesus as symbolic of the chosen relationship with God.
Not only is Jesus God's chosen son (consider the subtext of Isaac as
the one chosen for Abraham's unfulfilled sacrifice in Gen. 22), but he
also becomes the *actual* sacrifice whose blood becomes "the blood of
the covenant, shed for many for the forgiveness of sins" (Matt.
26:38; Mark 14:24). He is the "good shepherd" who will lead his
flock directly to God: "I am the door; anyone who comes into the
fold through me will be safe. He will go in and out and find pas-
ture.... I am the good shepherd; I know my own and my own knows
me, as the Father knows me and I know the Father" (John 10:9–15).

Those who follow the extraordinary and divinely chosen
Jesus gain a part of Jesus's extraordinary blessing. Their faith in
Jesus's incomparable merit actually brings a certain merit upon
them, and that merit includes a kind of personal election. Many
Greco-Romans and a few Jews, indeed, entered into the fold through
Jesus.

Most Jews, however, seem not to have followed him, yet they
nevertheless claimed to have the chosen status of Abraham's
descendents without following Jesus. They represent the establishment religion in the New Testament, and whether or not some Jews
actually intended to kill Jesus, there can be no doubt that they
opposed him vigorously. The Gospel of John accuses them of plot-
ting Jesus's death, and notes how they would cite their genealogical relationship with Abraham to prove their elect status. Jesus
turns the idiom of kinship relationship on its head by accusing
them, metaphorically, of acting as if they were children of the devil
rather than of Abraham.

"I know that you are descended from Abraham, yet you are bent on killing me because my teaching makes no headway with you. I tell what I have seen in my Father's presence; you do what you have learned from your father." They retorted, "Abraham is our father." "If you were Abraham's children," Jesus replied, "you would do as Abraham did. As it is, you are bent on killing me, because I have told you the truth, which I heard from God. That is not how Abraham acted. You are doing your own father's work." They said, "We are not illegitimate; God is our father, and God alone." Jesus said to them, "If God were your father, you would love me, for God is the source of my being, and from him I come. I have not come of my own accord; He sent me. Why do you not understand what I am saying? It is because my teaching is beyond your grasp. Your father is the devil and you choose to carry out your father's desires. He was a murderer from the beginning, and is not rooted in the truth; there is no truth in him. When he tells a lie he is speaking his own language, for he is a liar and the father of lies." (John 8:37–44)

By Jesus's day, conversion was both a possibility and a reality. In fact, many Greco-Romans who were neither Jewish nor Christian "shopped the market" during the first century CE and later in search of a more personally relevant religion. This was the largest potential pool of religious consumers, and some early church fathers noted in their writings how Greco-Romans listened to both Jewish and Christian leaders and attended various worship services.[2] Both rabbinic Judaism and Christianity represented newly emerging religious movements during the period, but because Judaism insisted that it was carrying the banner of biblical religion, Jews were also represented in the New Testament as the religious establishment, though the most powerful religious establishment was actually represented by the Roman state through worship of the emperor.

Primogeniture and Promise

If a new religious movement attacks the establishment head-on and aggressively, the polemical assault may not only cause it to suffer more from the results of direct confrontation, but it may also alienate potential followers who are considering their religious options before joining any movement. Successful new religious movements sometimes work subtly with authenticating symbols, therefore, and in ways that will accomplish the opposite of the desire of the establishment to denigrate them. In the following passage in Romans 11, for example, Paul starts off as if affirming the unique chosen status of Israel but then subverts that notion through a brilliant argument based on well-known biblical symbols and motifs:

> I ask then: Has God rejected his people? Of course not! I am an Israelite myself, of the stock of Abraham, of the tribe of Benjamin. God has not rejected the people he acknowledged of old as his own. Surely you know what scripture says in the story of Elijah—how he pleads with God against Israel: "Lord, they have killed your prophets, they have torn down your altars, and I alone am left, and they are seeking my life." But what was the divine word to him? "I have left myself seven thousand men who have not knelt to Baal." In just the same way at the present time a "remnant" has come into being, chosen by the grace of God. But if it is by grace, then it does not rest on deeds, or grace would cease to be grace. What follows? What Israel sought, Israel has not attained, but the chosen few have attained it. The rest were hardened.... I ask, then: When they stumbled, was their fall final? Far from it! Through a false step on their part salvation has come to the Gentiles, and this in turn will stir them to envy.... It is to you Gentiles that I am speaking. As an apostle to the Gentiles, I make much of that ministry, yet always in the hope of

stirring those of my own race to envy, and so saving some of them. For if their rejection has meant the reconciliation of the world, what will their acceptance mean? Nothing less than life from the dead! (Rom. 11:1–15)

A similar reworking of earlier symbols may be found in the same epistle:

Not all descendants of Israel are truly Israel, nor, because they are Abraham's offspring, are they all his true children; but in the words of Scripture, "Through the line of Isaac your descendants shall be traced" [Gen. 21:12]. That is to say, it is not those born in the course of nature who are children of God; it is the children born through God's promise who are reckoned as Abraham's descendants. (Rom. 9:7–8)

The critical subtext for this passage is Genesis 21:10–13:

She said to Abraham, "Cast out that slave-woman and her son, for the son of that slave shall not share in the inheritance with my son Isaac." The matter distressed Abraham greatly, for it concerned a son of his. But God said to Abraham, "Do not be distressed over the boy or your slave; whatever Sarah tells you, do as she says, for it is through the line of Isaac that your descendants shall be traced. As for the son of the slave woman, I will make a nation of him too, for he is your seed."

This is a critique of the Jewish claim of chosenness based on lineage. Paul's argument is that God's mysterious choice of Isaac over Ishmael for the covenantal chosen relationship is explained by the fact that earlier in the narrative, God promised that Abraham would have a second child, who would be named Isaac, through Sarah. Therefore, while Ishmael was indeed Abraham's firstborn son, he was simply a normal child, whereas Isaac was divinely promised and thus attained a preferred, chosen status. In the biblical system of primogeniture, a father's firstborn son served as the primary inheritor. Ishmael thus should have attained higher status than his younger brother, Isaac. And yet Isaac, who was born miraculously in Abraham and Sarah's old age and according to God's promise, was accorded higher status by God. According to this reading, simple genealogy is trumped by divine intent. In the same way, says Paul, the Jewish prior claim to chosenness based on direct blood-kinship with Abraham is trumped by the divine promise to those who follow Jesus as Christ-Messiah. The same analogy is made in an extremely powerful way in Galatians 4:21–31:

> Tell me now, you who are so anxious to be under the Law, will you not listen to what the Law says? It is written there that Abraham had two sons, one by his slave and the other by his free-born wife. The slave-woman's son was born in the course of nature, the free woman's through God's promise. This is an allegory. The two women stand for two covenants. The one bearing children into slavery is the covenant that comes from Mount Sinai: that is Hagar. Sinai is a mountain in Arabia and it represents the Jerusalem of today, for she and her children are in slavery. But the heavenly Jerusalem is the free woman; she is our mother! ... Now you, my friends, like Isaac, are children of God's promise, but just as in those days the natural-born son persecuted the spiritual son, so it is today. Yet what does scripture say? "Drive out the slave and her son, for the son of the slave shall not share the inheritance with the son of the free woman." [cf. Gen. 21:10] You see, then, my friends, we are no slave's children; our mother is the free woman. It is for freedom that Christ set us free. Stand firm, therefore, and refuse to submit again to the yoke of slavery.

The inheritance in this passage is the blessing of God through Jesus as Christ-Messiah. Inheritance is not simply attained by kinship relationship. It must be acquired through God's intentionality, and that intentionality is expressed through the very personhood of Jesus. Many other New Testament passages could be cited to show how important the competition was for being the real chosen of God. One of the most powerful and famous is the anonymous letter to the Hebrews 8:6–13, referenced above:

> In fact, the ministry which has fallen to Jesus is as far superior to [Israel's] as are the covenant he mediates and the promises upon which it is legally secured. Had the first covenant been faultless, there would have been no need to look for a second in its place. But God, finding fault with them, says, "The days are coming, says the Lord, when I will conclude a new covenant with the house of Israel and the house of Judah. It will not be like the covenant I made with their forefathers when I took them by the hand to lead them out of Egypt; because they did not abide by the terms of the covenant, and I abandoned them, says the Lord. For the covenant I will make with the house of Israel after those days, says the Lord, is this: I will set My laws in their understanding and write them on their hearts; and I will be their God, and they shall be My people. And they shall not teach one another, saying to brother and fellow-citizen, 'Know the Lord!' For all of them, high and low, shall know Me; I will be merciful to their wicked deeds, and I will remember their sins no more." By speaking of a new covenant, He has pronounced the first one old; and anything that is growing old and aging will shortly disappear.

The bulk of this passage is a citation of Jeremiah 31:31–34. Biblical scholars consider the Jeremiah passage to be part of a larger prophecy of consolation and restoration directed to the northern kingdom of Israel that had been destroyed by the Assyrians years earlier. The interpretation of the letter to the Hebrews is that the "new covenant" refers to one to be established between God and a new religious community that will replace the old. This is one of the powerful texts that claim the supersession of Christianity as the "true Israel" (the Latin phrase is *verus Israel*). In this passage the subtext of Jeremiah 31 is brought right into the text to demonstrate and strengthen the point. In the view expressed there, the new covenant represents a new dispensation, a new relationship between God and a replacement "chosen." The old claim to chosenness has no meaning because God has ended that relationship. The new chosen reflects the most perfect articulation of the divine will.

Chosenness as a Zero-sum Situation

The arguments that we have been reading reveal the view that the role of covenanted community was possible for one side only. In the language of game theory, the competition for divine election is depicted in these texts as a "zero-sum" situation: there can be only one elected, only one chosen at any time. If the Israelites are chosen, the Christians cannot be, and vice versa. Only one form of monotheism is valid.

That assumption was born in a period when the Israelites were the only community to arrive at the notion of monotheism. There *was* only one form of monotheism in the world of ancient Israel, or at least only one that could be known to them. The other expressions of monotheism or proto-monotheism mentioned above never survived. All other human communities and nations known to Israel were polytheists. Because the One Great God was "none of the above," meaning that God was not limited to being like a tribal god of any of the nations—and only Israel realized this—then only Israel could be chosen by the true God. There was only one chosen, and that chosen was Israel.

The notion of a single chosen is deeply embedded in the chosenness texts of the Hebrew Bible:

- Exodus 19:5–6: "You shall be My treasured possession among all the peoples, for all the earth is Mine."
- Leviticus 20:26: "I have set you apart from other peoples to be Mine."
- Deuteronomy 7:6: "The Lord your God chose you to be His treasured people."
- Deuteronomy 14:2: "The Lord your God chose you from among all other peoples on earth to be His treasured people."
- Isaiah 42:1: "This is My servant, whom I uphold, My chosen one, in whom I delight."

That notion of a single chosen became a dominant theme of Christianity as well, but the difference was that rather than being a religious peoplehood as in ancient Israel, and then rabbinic Judaism, the chosen in Christianity was a voluntary religious community, one of voluntary believers. But only those within that clearly defined community benefit from the new expression of divine election: "He who believes and is baptized shall be saved, but he who does not believe shall be condemned" (Mark 16:16).

Given the repeated statements of unique status, it is not surprising that the first two monotheistic religious systems to emerge out of the fall of the Jerusalem Temple agreed that there could only be one true monotheism. In our examination of Islam to follow, we will observe a somewhat different perception.

5

Chosenness and Covenant in the Qur'an

The Qur'an represents the divine message spoken by God through his angel Gabriel to Muhammad, who then recited the words he received to the people. In fact, the meaning of the word, *Qur'an,* is "recitation"—divine revelation delivered through the recitations of God's prophet Muhammad. The Qur'an emerges into history in the seventh century CE in the west-central Arabian region called the Hijaz.

Islam and the Religious Context of Arabia

The Roman Empire never controlled Arabia; neither did the Persian Empire or any other foreign power. Arabia remained outside the control of empire, but foreign cultures and religions nevertheless had a significant impact on community customs and the local way of life. The establishment religions that opposed the emergence of the new religious movement of Islam were three: Arabian polytheism, Judaism, and Christianity. Jews and Christians had lived in Arabia for centuries and had attracted local Arabs to join their religions through conversion. Arabian Jews and Christians were thus highly acculturated to the local language and cultural practices and functioned, for all intents and purposes, as Arabs practicing local versions of Judaism and Christianity.

73

Of the three establishment religious communities, the polytheists were the greatest obstacle to the emergence of Islam, and the
Qur'an directs its resentment and anger mostly toward the indigenous religion of the Arabs and those who practiced it. The most
common term for idolatry in the Qur'an is the word *shirk*, which
has the sense of "sharing, participating, associating." That term
carries something of the notion of polytheism known in the
Israelite world as well, since polytheists are assumed to associate
divinity in things other than God, and worship them in addition to
the deity. One who associates other powers with God is a *mushrik*.
Another term for those who did not follow Muhammad and accept
the validity of the Qur'an is *kafir*, which has the sense of "denying," as in denying the truth of God. This term has often been
translated as "infidel," though in modern Qur'an translations it is
more often translated as "unbeliever." When the Qur'an refers to
unbelievers, it may be referring to practitioners of traditional
Arabian polytheism *(mushriks)* or it may be referring to Jews and
Christians. The Qur'an notes that unbelievers tried actively to
destroy the new movement. "When you go forth in the land, it is
no sin to cut back in your prayers if you fear that the unbelievers
will attack you, for the unbelievers are clearly an enemy" (4:101).
This verse is followed with divine instruction about how to protect
the community that had been previously attacked while engaging
in prayer. This is followed by the words, "The unbelievers want
you to neglect your arms and your belongings so they may attack
you once and for all ... take precaution!" (4:102).

According to Islamic tradition, Muhammad began receiving
divine revelation in his hometown of Mecca, a major polytheistic religious center in his day. Beginning about the age of forty, he began to
receive revelations and continued to do so intermittently until his
death nearly twenty-three years later. He performed no miracles, but
his extraordinary charisma attracted many followers. His community
was dedicated to a simple ethical way of life under the authority of the
One Great God, the same God that had given prior revelation through
the Israelite prophets and Jesus. There is no evidence that there were

Jewish or Christian communities living in Mecca in the seventh century. The reason is most likely that they did not feel comfortable living in a center of polytheistic religious practice, though individuals would regularly go there in order to trade. On the other hand, there was a large Christian community living in the region called Najran to the south, and a large Jewish community living in Yathrib to the north. Mecca's status as religious center attracted tribes from throughout the region to make pilgrimage to it in order to worship the deities that were represented there by figures and pillars and images and temples. This was an important cultural and religious aspect of life in the region, and what we would call the "religious pilgrimage industry" was a mainstay of the Meccan economy.

Trading fairs rose up around Mecca during the height of the pilgrimage season, and entire extended families and clans would move into Mecca and the surrounding area for a number of days. They would go to the markets to trade, and they would need materials for sacrifices and guides to instruct them through the many varied rituals. When Muhammad began to attract followers to monotheism who then shunned the traditional religious practices in favor of simple prayer to the One Great God, he attracted the ire of the religious establishment. The threat was not merely one of competing religious ideology, but of competing business as well. The new religious movement soon grew large enough to represent a danger to the religious and the economic establishment of Mecca. He was vigorously opposed. The Qur'an contains passages that reproduce some of the accusations that were leveled against Muhammad by the polytheists of Mecca.

> So they were surprised that a warner has come to them from their midst. Those unbelievers say, "This is a lying conjuror! Has he made the deities into one God? This is indeed a strange thing!" The chiefs among them go around saying, "Go, and remain faithful to your gods. This is certainly something concocted. We have not heard such a thing among people recently. It is only a fabrication." (38:4–7)

God reassured Muhammad and supported him in his struggle. "And while the unbelievers plot against you to arrest you, kill you or drive you out, God plots too; and God is the better of the planners" (8:30). But Muhammad's status in Mecca continued to deteriorate and eventually became so precarious that his life was in danger. He needed to find refuge from the relentless harassment of the Meccan establishment that opposed him. An opportunity presented itself for him to move with his followers to the town of Yathrib, where Jews had a powerful presence. He agreed to make the move and in 622 CE he arrived in Yathrib, after which the town began to be called Medina, a shortened form of Madinat al-Nabi (City of the Prophet).

Competition and the "People of the Book"

Muhammad naturally expected the Jews of Medina to recognize his prophethood. After all, the idolatrous Meccans may have been hopelessly steeped in their worship of false gods, but it was well known in Arabia that the Jews were an ancient people with a history of prophets and revelations that were not unlike the revelations that he had received. Muhammad was sorely disappointed. From the perspective of the Jews, he was simply the leader of a threatening new religious movement. They accepted neither his prophetic teachings nor his prophetic status, just as their forebears in the Holy Land accepted neither the teachings nor the special status that Jesus claimed. Rather than an authentic prophet, Muhammad represented a threat to them and, unsurprisingly, they opposed him.

Jews and Christians are sometimes referred to in the Qur'an by Arabic translations of these names, but they are also referred to as "People of the Book." This term originates in the Qur'an, and it comes from the recognition that Jews and Christians were recipients of scripture before the revelation of the Qur'an. The Qur'an makes it quite clear that Jews and Christians were not happy with the presence of a new form of monotheism in their midst. "Many of the People of the Book would like to render you again unbelievers after your having believed, because of envy on their part after the truth has become clear to them. But forgive and be indulgent until God gives His command, for God is the Power over everything" (2:109). Because Muhammad lived in Medina where a large Jewish community had settled rather than in Najran or another area highly populated with Christians, most scholars believe that this and a number of similar verses are directed against Jews that he had encountered and who opposed him. This is also likely the reason why the Qur'an contains more criticism of Jews than Christians. Had Muhammad moved to a Christian area, the Christians would have opposed his claim to religious authority no less than the Jews. And in fact, in subsequent generations when Islam expanded beyond the Arabian peninsula, the Christian Byzantine Empire was the Muslims' most dangerous enemy, both as competing empire and as representative of competing religion.

Abraham and Authenticity

The Qur'an shares many symbols and ideas with the Hebrew Bible and the New Testament, and like them, it associates Abraham with its central symbols and religious values. Abraham is loyal, earnest, and witness to the absolute unity of God in the Qur'an, and he submits unceasingly to the divine will. Like the New Testament, the Qur'an provides its own answer to the mystery of why God chose Abraham. According to the Qur'an, Abraham's merit is found first in his ability to find God through reason. In polytheistic systems, celestial bodies such as the moon or stars and constellations were often worshiped. According to a passage in the Qur'an, as a young man, Abraham became attracted to the stars, which were soon eclipsed by the moon and then the brightness of the sun. When Abraham observed the cycle of rising and setting, he realized that one great creator must have brought them all into existence, and it is to that God that Abraham must turn (3:75–79).

The Qur'anic Abraham is the dedicated monotheist. He resisted the oppression of his own people in order to demonstrate the unity of God. He physically demolished the idols of his father and his people, and when they responded by threatening to kill him for destroying the idols, he fled in search of God (37:83–99). One cannot help but see the parallel between Muhammad's difficulties in Mecca and Abraham's stalwart insistence on monotheism despite the religious oppression of his own people. They both bring down the idols of their own community and are forced to flee for their devotion and commitment.

Abraham is depicted in the Qur'an as establishing the foundations of Islam's holiest shrine in Mecca along with his son Ishmael. This is consistent with his building of altars and sacred sites in the Holy Land according to the Bible (Gen. 12:7–8), and the Qur'an tells us that he prayed that his descendents be loyal to God and follow the ritual and theological requirements that would epitomize the religion of Islam.

And when Abraham and Ishmael were raising up the foundations of the House [they prayed]: "Our Lord, Accept [this] from us, for You are the Hearer, the Knower. Our Lord, Make us submitters [*muslimayn*] to You and our progeny a submissive people to You. Show us the ritual places and turn toward us, for You are the most relenting, the Merciful. Our Lord, send them a messenger from among them who will recite for them Your signs and teach them the Book and wisdom and make them pure and good. For You are the Mighty, the Wise." Who could dislike the religion of Abraham other than those who fool themselves? We have chosen him in [this] world. And in the hereafter, he is among the righteous. When the Lord said to him: Surrender [*aslim*]! He answered: "I surrender to the Lord of the universe." Abraham charged his sons, as did Jacob: "O my sons! God has chosen [the right] religion for you. [When you die,] die as submitters [to God]." (2:127–132)

Abraham proclaimed that God had chosen true religion, and that religion is represented in the passage with Abraham's devotion. The first thing that Abraham prayed for was that he and his descendents remain "submitters" to God. The Arabic term for one who surrenders or submits is *muslim*, and submission to God's will is a core principle of Islam. But even beyond the notion of submission as a key to Muslim identity is the symbolism of the actual word used to convey that notion. The difference in English transliteration between *muslim* as "submitter" and *Muslim* as a member of Islamic religion is conveyed by the use of lower- or uppercase letters. In Arabic, there are no lower- or uppercase forms, and therefore, no difference at all. Abraham, then, though he existed long before the emergence of Islam, represents the quintessential Muslim because he submitted fully to God. He symbolizes and authenticates some of the most iconic features of Islam in this passage: worship at the Ka'ba (House) in Mecca and submission to the divine will.

As in the Hebrew Bible and the New Testament, Abraham appears in the Qur'an as God's "friend." He thus represents for all three faith systems the pinnacle of relationship with God. "Who is better in religion than one who surrenders to God [using the same word, *muslim*] while being righteous and following the tradition of Abraham the monotheist. God chose Abraham as friend" (4:125).

Given Abraham's pivotal role as quintessential monotheist, it is not surprising that he figures deeply in Qur'anic polemic against not only polytheism, but also the establishment monotheisms of the day. When in another passage Abraham prays that his descendents receive the same blessings as him, God answers, "My covenant does not include wrongdoers" (2:124). This is a critique of Jewish claims to chosenness based on their kinship with Abraham, a critique that we also observed in the New Testament. The most striking example of Abraham's role in the polemics of all three expressions of monotheism, however, is in Qur'an 3:65–67:

> O People of Scripture! Why do you argue about Abraham, when the Torah and the Gospel were not revealed until after him? Have you no sense? Do you not argue about things of which you have knowledge? Why, then, argue about things of which you have no knowledge! God knows, but you know not! Abraham was not a Jew nor a Christian, but was a monotheist, a submitter [*muslim*], not an idolater.

In this one short passage, the Qur'an makes an end-run around Jewish and Christian claims in order to claim Abraham for Islam. According to the logic expressed here, Abraham could not have been a Jew or a Christian because the very definition for these two religious categories is based on the receipt of scriptural revelation. Jews are Jews because they follow the Torah, and Christians are Christians because they follow Jesus, whose mission is detailed in the Gospel. The definition of *muslim*, however, is simply "one who submits [to God]," and its meaning is not dependent on any scripture. Abraham was, by definition, a (small *m*) muslim because he submitted to the divine will. Since he lived before the revelations that would define Judaism and Christianity, he could not truly be claimed for either.

Whether a non-Muslim would agree with this argument or consider it merely an issue of semantics, the point here is that Abraham becomes a symbol of the natural competition between newly emerging religions and establishment religions. He appears in the important role of legitimizing each religious system because he so powerfully represents the relationship between God and humanity. And as we have observed, he appears in all three scriptures in roles that endorse some very specific and particular traits of each religion. When the three are compared, however, we cannot help but find that he authenticates religions that have different, even conflicting views on some of the most basic issues. Abraham, therefore, is not exactly the same person in the three scriptures. In the Hebrew Bible he represents ultimate obedience to the divine call despite his occasional doubt (as in Gen. 17:17–18). In the New

Testament he symbolizes absolute faith in God even before he was called, and thus serves as a role model for the necessary faith in Christ. And in the Qur'an Abraham authenticates the sanctity of Islamic religious practice and epitomizes the need for humanity to submit humbly to the will of God. His role as God's chosen, God's love or intimate friend, makes him the veritable symbol of right religion for each religious tradition. His character and personality thus become central and basic to each as a means of authentication and legitimization.

Qur'anic expressions of the chosenness of Islam are not dependent only on the figure of Abraham. Plenty of other expressions may be found to demonstrate God's choice as well. For example, in a discussion on permitted foods that finds some parallels with the dietary laws found in the Hebrew Bible is the statement, "This day I have perfected your religion for you, completed My favor upon you, and have chosen for you Islam as your religion" (5:3). And in a reproof directed against the People of the Book who were harassing the new community of believers, God assures Muhammad's followers, "You are the best community that has been brought forth for humanity, commanding the reputable and forbidding the disreputable, and believing in God. If the People of the Book had believed it would have been better for them. Some of them are believers, but most are degenerate" (3:110).

In this passage, the elite status that is conveyed upon the new community of believers is dependent on engaging in proper behaviors. In the following passage it is the combination of proper behavior and proper faith that merits the inheritance of the special status previously reserved for others. "God has promised those of you who believe and do good works that He will make them heirs of the land, just as He made those before them to be heirs, and He will surely establish for them their religion that He has approved for them, exchanging security for them in place of fear. They shall worship Me and not associate anything with Me. Those who disbelieve after that are the reprobate" (24:55). The message here is consistent with the repeated Qur'anic critique of the earlier covenants.

Membership within a covenanted community is never static in the Qur'an. You must validate your membership through belief and action, a criterion that allows for Muslims to inherit the status of Jews and Christians, who are accused of neglecting or abandoning the requirements that were earlier placed upon them.

Supersession or Correction?

These passages illustrate how concerned the Qur'an is with the covenantal claims of Jews and Christians. But it does not claim to supersede them as the New Testament claims to supersede the "old" covenant of the Hebrew Bible. The Qur'an certainly excludes most Jews and Christians from the very covenants they claim to represent and uphold by citing their lack of commitment to them (2:124, 4:54–55, 5:12–14), but it does not claim to replace them. Rather, it claims to "correct" them and to provide a means of bringing errant monotheists (not to mention polytheists!) back to the proper path to God. Abraham, for example, epitomized the true monotheist who submitted himself fully to God's will. According to the Qur'an, most Jews and Christians have lost sight of the true essence of the Abrahamic commitment.

Despite the passages that claim to represent Islam as God's chosen religion and its followers as God's chosen community, the Qur'an is not actually as preoccupied with the chosenness issue as the Hebrew Bible and the New Testament are. Recall that the competition for chosen status between Jews and Christians was a "zero-sum" situation based on the unique nature of monotheism in a world that was overwhelmingly polytheistic. It was inconceivable in that environment to think that there could be more than one divinely chosen community. Jews and Christians at the time argued over which one was the chosen one.

By the seventh century, however, much had changed in the Near East. The Roman Empire had become the Christian Byzantine Empire, and Jews and Christians had become increasingly dispersed throughout the region. These two developments encouraged a huge influx of erstwhile polytheists into one or another of these two monotheistic systems. Moreover, Christianity had produced many different expressions and denominations, and Judaism also existed in a variety of forms between the Holy Land, Mesopotamia, and Egypt. Historical demographers believe that the overwhelming majority of peoples in the Near East at this time were monotheists of one form or another, while a significant minority was represented by Zoroastrianism. Zoroastrianism is an ancient religious system that emerged independently of either Judaism or Christianity, and it is not monotheistic. Nevertheless, it was the state religion of the Persian Empire and was extremely sophisticated and impressive, represented by great literatures and theologies, administered by a highly educated priesthood, and organized around beautiful temples and monumental structures. All three great religious systems represented high religious civilization in relation to the old, indigenous polytheisms. In fact, only a few pockets of traditional polytheism remained in the Near East at this time. The largest seems to have been in Arabia.

In other words, it was no longer so unique in the Near East of the late seventh century to believe in the One Great God. Even Arabia had a well-known population of monotheists, and when Arabs traded beyond the borders of Arabia, most of the people they came into contact with were monotheists as well. Islam was thus born in a world that was radically different from either the world of emerging biblical monotheism or the world of emerging Christianity. As Islam emerged into its own religious world, its devotees could not claim exclusive truth as monotheists in a world of polytheism, as did ancient Israel. Neither could they claim sole possession of the ultimate relationship with the One Great God in a simple bilateral competition with the Jews, as did Christianity. The new Muslim community encountered a multi-monotheist playing field in which the goal had to be, simply, to demonstrate superiority in its claim for share of the market. The religious fellowship of Islam, the *umma* in Qur'anic parlance as articulated in Qur'an 3:110, is "the best community that has been brought forth for humanity," but only as long as its members would "command the reputable and forbid the disreputable, and believe in God."

Exactly what was meant by these requirements was not articulated unambiguously in the Qur'an. That is to say, would successfully fulfilling these three obligations be possible only within an Islamic framework? Or could Jews and Christians acceptably command the reputable and forbid the disreputable within their own religious systems? Some Qur'anic passages, such as 2:62, say that they may: "Those who believe, and who are Jews, and Christians and Sabaeans—whoever believes in God and the Last Day and who work righteousness—they have their reward with their Lord, they shall not fear nor should they grieve." The identical message is given again in 5:69, and although debatable, 22:17 might even include Zoroastrians among those approved by God.

Other verses, such as 9:29, take a different position, which according to many interpreters is considered to have abrogated the more welcoming verses mentioned above. "Fight those given scripture who do not believe in God or in the Last Day and do not make forbidden what God and His messenger have made forbidden, and do not practice the religion of truth, until they pay tribute willingly, in a humbled state." This verse may be interpreted as condemning only those People of the Book who are not true to their own scriptural traditions, or it may be interpreted to mean that all those who have been given prior scripture have become unbelievers and rebels against the very divine revelation that they received. However one may interpret this verse, it places monotheists represented by the religions of the book in a secondary position to Muslims. It is an elitist position, but it is not supersessionist. Even in exclusivist readings of the Qur'an, chosenness is shared among all monotheists. In theory, at least, there is a place for the covenanted chosenness of Judaism and Christianity within Islam.

6

Chosenness and Covenant in Rabbinic Literature

The Claim for Continuity

As mentioned previously, rabbinic Judaism represents a new expression of biblical religion, but unlike either Christianity or Islam, it never claimed that status. Its position, rather, was that it *was* biblical religion, but with some adjustments after the Roman destruction of its Temple in Jerusalem, and therefore, the forced termination of its ancient mode of worshiping God through animal sacrifice. Rather than claim a new dispensation as did Christianity, or a correction of the errors of the old as did Islam, rabbinic Judaism claimed continuity with the original and authentic monotheism represented by Abraham and the biblical patriarchs, Moses at Mount Sinai, David and Solomon, who built up Jerusalem and established God's Temple there, and the great prophets of Israel.

Judaism, therefore, was not static but continued to evolve, and its evolution included the emergence of a body of literature in the Talmud that was so deeply linked with the scripture of the Bible that it developed a scriptural status itself. The emergence of the Talmud took centuries. Its earliest parts date from a century or more before Jesus, and its end-date was in the period shortly before the Arab Muslim conquest of the seventh century. The

Talmud is so thoroughly integrated with the Hebrew Bible that the biblical subtext of any passage is usually included as part of the text itself. This can be observed quite clearly in the passages that treat chosenness.

The following section from the Talmud (Avodah Zarah 2a–b) is fully caught up in the argument over who best merits God's love for living out the divine will, and who best merits God's reward for doing so:

> In times to come the Holy One will bring a Torah scroll, embrace it to His chest and say, "Whoever has been occupied with this come forth and receive its reward!" Immediately, all the idolaters will gather together in confusion, as it is said (Isaiah 43:9), *All the nations gathered together.* The Holy One will say to them, "Do not gather before Me in confusion. Let each nation enter separately with its scribes, as it is said (in the continuation of Isaiah 43:9), *and let the peoples be gathered together....* The Holy One will say to [the Romans who come first], "How have you been occupying yourselves?" They will answer, "Lord of the Universe, we have established many marketplaces, we have built many baths, we have accumulated much gold and silver. We did this only [to support the Jews] so that they could devote themselves to the study of Torah." The Holy One will reply, "You fools! All that you did was only for your own sake. You have established marketplaces to provide whores, baths to revel with them, and as for the silver and gold, it is Mine, as it is written (Hag. 2:8), *The silver and the gold are Mine, says the Lord of Hosts.*

Then the Persians step forward and make the case for carrying out God's design by supporting the Jews so that they can live out God's will. But they, too, are chastised for being selfish and thinking only of themselves. All the nations do likewise and all are invalidated for not personally taking responsibility for engaging in Torah as did the Jews. The nations then argue a different position to God. "But [the Gentiles] will argue, 'How can You blame us for not carrying out the Torah when we never agreed to accept it?' The response that follows is, 'Then why did you not accept it?'" The passage then goes on to state that the other nations took on the responsibility to observe a much reduced version of the Torah that the Talmud refers to as "the Seven Commandments given to Noah," but even these they failed to obey. The chosen status of the Jews is thus proven through the invalidation of all other communities.

This is an interesting passage for a number of reasons. First, it serves as a consolation to the Jews, who had suffered the destruction of the Temple, dispersion into exile, and insult and mistreatment after the ascendance of Christianity. How could they continue to see themselves as God's favored people when they are in such straits and their competitors the Christians seem to bask in the light of God after the Christianization of the Roman Empire in the fourth century? Christianity is not openly condemned in this passage, but it was dangerous for a despised and powerless minority to criticize the religion of the empire. *Rome,* therefore, became a code word for "Christianity" in rabbinic literature because the Roman Empire did Christianize. It should also be noted that after Christianity became the religion of the empire, Jews had to self-censure their criticism of Christians to protect themselves.

Chosenness as Consolation

Many Talmudic passages that treat Israel's chosenness are forms of consolation. The following conveys two reassuring messages about the important role of the Jews for the world's well-being:

> Resh Lakish said, Why is there an additional letter *"hey"* in *It was evening and then morning,* the *sixth day* (Gen. 1:31)?[1] This teaches that the Holy One stipulated with the works of Creation by saying to them, "If Israel accepts the Torah,

you will exist, but if not I will turn you back into emptiness and formlessness." (Shabbat 88a)

The first message is to the Jews, and it tells them to hold fast to their religion, despite their humiliation, for God is willing to keep the world in existence only on account of Israel's loyalty to God through observing the Torah. That is to say, Israel is still God's chosen despite the Jews' current degradation. The second message is directed to the entire world, including those who are in superior political and social position to the Jews. That message asserts that the very existence of those who degrade the Jews is ironically dependent upon the Jews whom they despise. Of course, that audience is not reading this text anyway, so the message is really directed internally. It provides Jews hope for a day in which God will redeem them from their unhappy state.

It should be noted that rabbinic literature in the Talmud and related literatures is a large collection of tradition. Various positions and opinions are presented in ways that are not intended to be absolutely consistent, so anyone reading through the material will observe differing positions on many issues and variant interpretations of biblical verses. In one series of biblical interpretations, it is maintained that God loves Israel even more than God loves the divine angels. A rabbinic midrash (exposition) from the eighth century cites many cases from the Bible where the same word refers to Israel and to God's angels. With poetic symmetry, the work sets out to prove that the ways in which those words are used shows that God loves his chosen people Israel even more than his angelic servants:[2]

> Israel is called "servants," as it is said, *For to Me Israel are servants* (Lev. 25:55), and the ministering angels are called servants, as it is said, *And if He cannot trust His own servants (and casts reproach on His angels)* (Job 4:18). How do you know who is more beloved? [God] says, *They are my servants whom I freed from the land of Egypt* (Lev. 25:55).

Israel, you are more beloved to Me than the ministering angels.

Israel is called "children," as it is said, *You are children of the Lord your God* (Deut. 14:1), and the ministering angels are called "children," as it is said, *The children of divine beings came to God* (Job 1:6). How do you know who is more beloved? [God] says, *Israel is My firstborn son* (Exod. 4:22).[3] Israel, you are more beloved to Me than the ministering angels.

Israel is called "kings" ... and the ministering angels are called "kings" ... Israel, you are more honored by Me than the ministering angels.

Israel is called "hosts" and the ministering angles are called "hosts" ... Israel, you are greater to Me than the ministering angels.

Israel is called "holy" and the ministering angels are called "holy" ... Israel, you are more holy to Me than the ministering angels.

This exegesis sets out to show how God could not possibly have stopped loving Israel. Israel is more beloved to God even than the ministering angels, thus showing God's love for the Jews as unique and everlasting. This consolation takes on particular meaning as we observe how the positions of Jews and Christians were reversed in the fourth century. Judaism had been favored by the pagan Roman Empire early on, while Christianity was brutally persecuted. Subsequently, both Jews and Christians represented threats to the empire and both were persecuted. But when the empire Christianized, the tables were completely turned. With that change, Christianity represented the establishment religion, after which Judaism was depicted by Christians as a despised religion.

Rabbi Elazar Ben Azaria ... said, *You have affirmed this day that the Lord is your God ... and the Lord has affirmed this*

day that you are, as He promised you, His treasured peo-
ple (Deut. 26:17–18). The Holy One said to Israel, "You
have made Me the sole object of your love and I have made
you the sole object of My love. You have made Me the
sole object of love, as it is written, *Hear O Israel, the Lord
our God is One* (Deut. 6:4). And I will make you the
sole object of love, as it is said, *Who is like Your people,
Israel, a unique nation on earth* (1 Chron. 17:21). (Talmud,
Hag. 3a–b)

In the rabbinic model, therefore, despite the profound decline
of the Jews with the destruction of the beloved Jerusalem Temple
and their persecution by the pagan Roman Empire, their institu-
tionalized discrimination by the Christianized Roman Empire of
Byzantium, and the dispersion of Jews throughout the
Mediterranean world and beyond, God never rejected His "chosen
people." The Jews never lost their exceptional status. Although they
may continue to suffer, their suffering is a suffering of love (*yis-
surey ahavah*) that would end in some unknown future when the
true messiah will come to redeem Israel, and through that redemption, redeem the entire world.

7

The Merit of the Ancients

The competition for divine election was articulated in various ways by the three great religious civilizations. The bottom line of chosenness is the question of which community is most beloved in the eyes of God. Whom does God love most? And, therefore, which community receives more of God's blessings? Ultimately, the best religious community is the one that understands God best, the community that knows the divine imperative. Understanding God requires knowing God's nature and expectations, and this is usually explained through theology. Theology is concerned with such questions as, how do we know what God expects of us? What do we know about God's nature, and how do we know it? These are old questions, but they continue to be relevant in every generation. These and related questions are reformulated and articulated by religious leaders and educators in ways that respond to the changing circumstances of the times, and they are often formulated and answered in a manner that reflects the competition among religions. We are not interested here in the details of formal theology, but there are other ways that religions have argued over which community merits more of God's special blessing.

Blessing by Association

One of the more interesting ways of arguing the relative value of the three monotheistic systems is by claiming special, divine merit associated with their most saintly members. This is a very ancient notion. It suggests at its core that the best people represent the best community, so those who can prove that their leaders and progenitors are the most righteous and saintly thereby prove that they belong to the most righteous and saintly community. It also suggests at a very simple level that hanging around a great person will cause some of the greatness to rub off on the follower. The desire for "blessing by association" helps explain why so many people love to see great athletes, movie stars, or political leaders in person. There is a deep-seated feeling that we will somehow pick up some of the stardust of those exceptional people, that somehow we may gain a little status and merit from the connection.

Many religions, including the three families of monotheism, contain the notion of "merit of the ancients." According to this idea, the special merit of saintly ancestors or previous religious leaders can benefit their religious followers. It does not rub off from personal experience, of course, because the righteous people, saints, or holy individuals from whom merit may be absorbed or acquired have long since passed on. It is possible, nevertheless, to benefit from the righteousness of those before us and to receive some of their blessing. How does this happen? One way to think about it is to think about our own personal merit. All religions include the notion that God appreciates us for being good. Although reward for our goodness may not be realized in this world, we assume that there will be an eventual payoff, at least in a world to come.

But we all have our foibles. Even more, we are weak and vulnerable to temptation and sin. If we are truly honest with ourselves, we realize that we are probably not really good enough. We know in our hearts that we fail repeatedly to be as good as we should, or as we *could*. We succumb to temptation, to selfishness and greed.

We find reasons why we should not go out of our way to help others. We are often jealous. We envy our neighbors and coworkers. There are thousands of ways that we know we don't live up to our potential to do the right thing and be good. We rely on God's compassion and mercy to forgive us for our sins. But why should God show compassion to us, who are so riddled with failings and wrongdoings?

God has sympathy toward us in part because God is understood in all monotheistic religions to be inherently compassionate and understanding. But there is more to God's mercy than simple benevolence. After all, God is depicted in the Bible and the Qur'an in the role of a severe and righteous judge as well as a gentle and kind parent, and honest justice might require that we be punished severely for our sins. We would inevitably fail the test if we were judged impartially and with strict justice. But there is a special advantage in the merit of our pious forbears. The three religious systems of Judaism, Christianity, and Islam each understands that the remarkable saintliness of certain people can "rub off" and can be counted for righteousness among others who are not so saintly.

The virtue, piety, and godliness of these extraordinary people have so much merit in the eyes of God that it spills over and becomes a gift for following generations. The most famous example of this notion is in the merit of Jesus in Christianity. Jesus's extraordinary love, righteousness, suffering, and death brought so much merit to the world that all humanity can be redeemed through him. It is Jesus's ultimate act of selflessness that trumps our selfishness, his righteousness that exceeds our injustices, his love that overcomes our resentment and hatred. This notion is not limited to Christianity, however. It is important in Judaism and Islam as well (though not through Jesus), and it functions as a way for Muslims and Jews to receive help in attaining divine forgiveness and atonement, and in achieving a place in heaven in the world to come.

In Judaism, the term that describes this sense of associative merit is *zekhut avot*, which means, literally, "merit of the ancestors."

The same basic notion became central to Christianity's theology of salvation through the concept of divine grace. Islam also retains something of this notion, although the Qur'an is careful to clarify that every individual is judged by God according to his or her own merits (39:41 and chapter 56). Although less developed in formal Islamic theology, benefiting from the righteous merit of others still remains a powerful religious impulse among Muslims. Some find support for it in the Qur'an: "There can be no intercession except by God's permission" (10:3).

In addition to the overflow of merit of the righteous ancients, each of the three systems also includes the possibility of appealing for intercession through saintly individuals whose extraordinary merit enables them to act as advocates on our behalf. Although the notion of the availability of extra merit from righteous predecessors exists in all three religious systems, each one understands it and works it out in somewhat different ways. One thing they have in common, however, is the inclination to understand that the benefit of extra merit applies exclusively to fellow believers. Those outside the faith system will not benefit from the merit of the pious forebears.

Merit of the Ancestors in Judaism

In Judaism, merit of the ancestors is limited almost entirely to Jews. There are a few references to non-Jews receiving merit from pious Gentiles, such as the righteous Noah, but they are few. From the period of the Bible onward, the religion of Israel has been organized around a peoplehood, *am yisra'el* (People of Israel). We have noted previously that Judaism has never been racially or ethnically limited. In the Exodus out of Egyptian slavery, many oppressed peoples made their escape along with the Israelites and took on the responsibilities of the divine covenant at Mount Sinai along with the tribes of Israel. And different national communities inter-married with the Israelites from the earliest times as well. Joseph married an Egyptian (Gen. 41:45), Moses married a Midianite (Exod. 2:15–22), King David's ancestors included Moabites

(Ruth 1:4, 4:13–21), and Solomon married many non-Israelite women (1 Kings 11:1–3)! But because religion in the ancient Near East was *organized* tribally, the sense of being Jewish has often been articulated in language that feels ethnic, even though Jews derive from all races and ethnic groups from Ethiopia and Uganda to India, China, Europe, and Native America. The multiethnic, multiracial community that is Israel remains nevertheless unique in its religious peoplehood, and in the Jewish view, the benefits of ancestral merit are limited to that extended community.

The Jewish notion of merit of the ancestors is founded on verses of promise to the biblical patriarchs that they would be rewarded through their offspring for their exceptional merit in responding to God's command. "By myself I swear, the Lord declares: Because you have done this and have not withheld your son, your favored one, I will bestow My blessing upon you and make your descendants as numerous as the stars of heaven and the sands on the seashore; and your descendants shall seize the gates of their foes. All the nations of the earth shall bless themselves by your descendants, because you have obeyed My command" (Gen. 22:16–18). In the next two generations, Isaac and then Jacob receive similar blessings of promise for their own offspring (Gen. 26:1–5 and Gen. 28:10–14).

Many generations later, after the Children of Israel had been redeemed from the bondage of Egyptian slavery and were living in the desert, the merit of the ancestors saved them from certain death. This is the story of the golden calf (Exodus 32). After Moses tarried on Mount Sinai for forty days and forty nights, the people became restless and reverted to the old habit of constructing an object through which they could direct their prayers. This was explicitly forbidden in the Ten Commandments (Exod. 20:4), and God was furious with their quick reversion to pagan ways. God warned Moses to stand aside, as God would destroy the Israelites for their sin. But Moses pleaded with God to spare them, and he based his defense on God's earlier promise to reward the patriarchs' children on account of their merit:

Moses implored the Lord his God, saying, "Let not Your anger, O Lord, blaze forth against Your people, whom You delivered from the land of Egypt with great power and with a mighty hand.... Turn from Your blazing anger, and renounce the plan to punish Your people. Remember Your servants, Abraham, Isaac, and Jacob, how You swore to them by Your Self and said to them: I will make your offspring as numerous as the stars of heaven, and I will give to your offspring the whole land of which I spoke, to possess forever." And the Lord renounced the punishment He had planned to bring upon His people. (Exod. 32:11–14)

These biblical foundations are extended in rabbinic literature. In the world of the Rabbis, the extraordinary merit of the biblical patriarchs and matriarchs was so great that it could be counted on to sustain their descendants in time of need. It works something like a savings account, although this is not the image employed by the Jewish sages (there were no such things in those days!). When times are good and we have more than we need to sustain ourselves, we deposit the extra in a bank account and save it for when we might need it. If we are particularly prudent, we are able to accumulate a savings that we can pass down to our children so they can use it when they might be in need. In the case of saintly ancestors, their merit was so extraordinary that it spilled over and accumulated in a kind of heavenly account. For the extremely righteous, their merit is so vast that it can be drawn upon by their children and their children's children.

The Rabbis of the Talmud would cite the Torah as support for their belief that the penance and atonement of the Jews would be accepted by God because of the merit of their righteous ancestors: "And they shall atone for their iniquity. Then will I remember My covenant with Jacob; I will remember also My covenant with Isaac, and also My covenant with Abraham; and I will remember the land ... while they atone for their iniquity.... I will not reject them or spurn them so as to destroy them, annulling My covenant with them: for I the Lord am their God. I will remember in their favor the covenant with the ancients, whom I freed from the land of Egypt in the sight of the nations to be their God: I, the Lord" (Lev. 26:41–45).

According to the Rabbis, it was not only the merit of the patriarchs that atoned, but the merit of the matriarchs as well. "Rabbi Ami said, Why is [the account of] the death of Miriam placed next the story of the Red Heifer?[1] To teach you that, just as the Red Heifer provided atonement, so does the death of the righteous provide atonement" (Babylonian Talmud, Mo'ed Qatan 28a). The Rabbis of the Talmud considered the righteous merit of Abraham to have truly extraordinary power. It was on account of his merit that God parted the Red Sea for the Israelites in their Exodus from Egypt: "The faith that father Abraham entrusted in Me is sufficient for Me to split the sea for them, as it is said, *And he believed in the Lord; and He counted it to him for righteousness* (Gen. 15:6)."[2] The merit of the ancestors is so great that it will never be used up: "Rabbi Aha said: Merit of the ancestors will exist forever. We shall always mention it and say, *for the Lord your God is a compassionate God: He will not fail you nor will He let you perish; He will not forget the covenant of your ancestors* (Deut. 4:31)."[3]

During droughts and times of fear, the Rabbis offered special prayers that appealed to God to forgive the failings of the Jews and provide rain or safety based on the merit of the ancestors. The following is a very old prayer based on the merit of many righteous biblical characters. It dates from around the first century CE:

After the first [special benediction recited on fast days], the prayer leader recites, "He who answered Abraham on Mt. Moriah, may He answer you and hearken to the voice of your crying this day, Blessed are You, O Eternal, Redeemer of Israel." After the second he recites, "He who answered our ancestors at the Red Sea, may He answer you and hear the voice of your crying this day, Blessed are You, O Eternal, who remembers those things forgotten." After the third he recites, "He who answered Joshua at Gilgal, may

He answer you and hearken to the voice of your crying this day. Blessed are You, O Eternal, who hears the sound of the Shofar." After the fourth he recites, "He who answered Samuel in Mitzpah, may He answer you and hear the voice of your crying this day. Blessed are You, O Eternal, who hears crying out." After the fifth he recites, "He who answered Elijah on Mt. Carmel, may He answer you and hearken to the voice of your crying this day. Blessed are You, O Eternal, who hears prayer." After the sixth, he recites, "He who answered Jonah from the belly of the fish, may He answer you and hear the voice of your crying. Blessed are You, O Eternal, who answers in time of distress." After the seventh he recites, "He who answered David and Solomon his son in Jerusalem, may He answer you and hearken to the voice of your crying this day. Blessed are You, O Eternal, who has compassion on the land." (Mishnah Ta'anit 2:4)

Notwithstanding the great number of biblical characters from which merit may be derived, the greatest example of ancestral merit in Judaism is the story of Abraham and Isaac's willingness to go along with God's command to Abraham to sacrifice his son. This is known as the Akedah (Binding) in Judaism. In the following two rabbinic readings of Genesis 22, Abraham and Isaac, and even the redemptive ram sacrificed in place of Abraham's son, accrue merit that can be withdrawn in future generations:

Rabbi Bibi Abba said in the name of Rabbi Yohanan: Abraham said before the Holy One, "Master of the worlds, it is revealed and known to you that when you told me to offer my son Isaac I could have responded and said to you, 'Yesterday you told me that Isaac would be called my seed (Gen. 21:12), and now you tell me to offer him as a burnt offering, heaven forbid?!' But I did not [respond negatively]. Rather, I suppressed my inclination and did Your will. So be it Your will, my Lord God, that when Isaac's children enter into trouble and have no one to plead their case, that You defend them. *O Lord who will see* (Gen. 22:14), remember for them the binding of Isaac their ancestor and be filled with compassion for them!" What is written afterwards? *And Abraham lifted up his eyes and saw another ram* (Gen. 22:13). What is *another (achar)*? Rabbi Yuda son of Rabbi Simon, "After *(achar)* all the future generations, your children will be caught up in sins and will be entangled in troubles, but in the end they will be redeemed with the horns of that ram, as it is said, *The Lord God will sound the ram's horn in a stormy tempest* (Zechariah 9:14).[4]

Rabbi Huna in the name of Rabbi Hinena bar Yitzhak: That entire day Abraham saw the ram caught in a tree and then get released, and become caught in a wood, then become released and go and get caught in a bush, then get released and go out [again]. The Holy One said to Abraham, "Thus in the future your children will get caught up in sins and become entangled among the nations, from Babylonia to Media, from Media to Greece, from Greece to Rome." [Abraham] said before Him: "Master of the worlds, that is the way it will always be?" [God] replied, "They will be redeemed in the end by the horns of that ram: *The Lord God will sound the ram's horn in a stormy tempest* (Zechariah 9:14). (Jerusalem Talmud, Ta'anit 2 [65d])

Who benefits from the merit of the ancestors? We have already seen that the answer is the extended descendants of the ancestors. Those who are not a part of the religious community of Israel (including both biological descendents and those who have chosen to become part of the community) do not benefit from the merit of the righteous of Israel. The notion of merit of the ancestors is internal, particular, and closed. Only those who are a part of the chosen people may benefit from this extraordinary merit.

Divine Grace in Christianity

In Christianity, the power of the parallel concept would appear to be far greater than in Judaism, but it is also narrowly limited to the religious community of believers. In a second parallel with Judaism, Christianity associates God's grace with a sacrifice that occurs in fascinating congruence with the Akedah (Binding) in Judaism: the crucifixion of Jesus.

The Christian term for God's command to Abraham to sacrifice his son is not the Binding, as it is in Judaism, but the Sacrifice. In Judaism, the merit derives from the willingness to obey the divine command. In Christianity, greater merit is said to have accrued from its actualization. The Sacrifice of Isaac was not carried out, of course, but it became a precursor in Christianity for the actual sacrifice of God's own son Jesus. According to most Christian thinking, God sent Jesus to make atonement for the sins of humankind through his crucifixion and subsequent resurrection. This was an act of God's grace freely given on behalf of all of humanity, but there remains a sense of obedience in the sacrifice as well. This tension can be seen clearly in the Gospel of John, where Jesus says, "I lay down my life to receive it back again. No one takes it away from me; I am laying it down of my own free will" (John 10:18), "The world must be shown that I love the Father and am doing what He commands" (John 14:31). Because Jesus as the incarnation of God is far more powerful than the mortal Abraham and Isaac, the merit that accrues for his selfless act is far greater than theirs and able to redeem far more people than the limited community of Israel. Neither restricted to the Jews or even to Jesus's followers, the merit is available to all humankind.

Most Christians agree that humanity is born in a state of sin, a consequence of the original sin and resulting fall of Adam and Eve in the Garden of Eden (1 Cor. 15:22; Rom. 5:14–15). The terrible sin that the first man and woman committed works as a kind of reverse merit that is then passed down to all humanity, through each generation. Every person is personally blighted by the overwhelming nature of that original sin; every individual is therefore born in sin. No good works or righteous acts can overcome the stain of that original sin.[5] Humanity is therefore born having forfeited any claim to salvation. It is *only* through the redemption bought by Jesus's willing self-sacrifice that anyone is saved, and the path of salvation for humanity lies in participating in that redemption through faith.

> I discover this principle, then: that when I want to do right, only wrong is within my reach. In my inmost self I delight in the law of God, but I perceive in my outward actions a different law, fighting against the law that my mind approves, and making me a prisoner under the law of sin which controls my conduct. Wretched creature that I am, who is there to rescue me from this state of death? Who but God? Thanks be to Him through Jesus Christ our Lord! To sum up then: left to myself I serve God's law with my mind, but with my unspiritual nature I serve the law of sin. (Rom. 7:21–25)

> Christ died for us while we were yet sinners, and that is God's proof of his love towards us. And so, since we have now been justified by Christ's sacrificial death, we shall all the more certainly be saved through him from final retribution. For if, when we were God's enemies, we were reconciled to him through the death of his Son, how much more, now that we have been reconciled, shall we be saved by his life! But that is not all: we also exult in God through our Lord Jesus, through whom we have now been granted reconciliation. What does this imply? It was through one man that sin entered the world, and through sin death, and thus death pervaded the whole human race, inasmuch as all have sinned.... But God's act of grace is out of all proportion to Adam's wrongdoing. For if the wrongdoing of that one man brought death upon so many, its effect is vastly exceeded by

the grace of God and the gift that came to so many by the grace of one man, Jesus Christ. It follows, then, that as the result of one misdeed was condemnation for all people, so the result of one righteous act is acquittal and life for all. For as through the disobedience of one man many were made sinners, so through the obedience of one man many will be made righteous. (Rom. 5:8–19)

At first sight, the Christian system of merit described in these passages appears to be inclusive, as opposed to the exclusive system of Judaism. But the atonement from sin with its resultant salvation is only possible for those who belong to the community of Christ. Only the new chosen may be saved. Only those who believe in the saving power of Christ can be saved by his merit.

But God is rich in mercy, and because of His great love for us, He brought us to life with Christ when we were dead because of our sins; it is by grace you are saved. And He raised us up in union with Christ Jesus and enthroned us with him in the heavenly realms, so that He might display in the ages to come how immense are the resources of His grace, and how great His kindness to us in Christ Jesus. For by Grace you have been saved through faith; it is not your own doing. It is God's gift. (Eph. 2:4–8)

In Christian parlance, God's grace means God's loving favor despite humanity's inability to transcend the stain of original sin. It is by God's grace that salvation is granted to humankind. But there is a stipulation, a requirement that must be fulfilled in order to benefit from the merit. That condition is faith in Jesus as Lord and Savior, conviction that Jesus is from God, trust that he is the Messiah, and confidence that his death on the cross has the power to take away human sins.

Only those who are true Christians can thus benefit from divine grace in the Christian system. "Remember the terms in which

I preached the gospel to you—for I assume that you hold it fast and that your conversion was not in vain. First and foremost, I handed on to you the tradition I had received: that Christ died for our sins, in accordance with the scriptures; that he was buried; that he was raised to life on the third day, in accordance with the scriptures, and that he appeared to Cephas, and afterwards to the Twelve. Then he appeared to over five hundred of our brothers at once" (1 Cor. 15).

Human and Divine Intercession in Islam

We have already noted how Islam emerged in a world in which competing expressions of monotheism were engaged in heated polemics over who had the exclusive chosen relationship with God. Jews and Christians agreed that there was a single divine covenant and that those counted within the covenant derived special status and benefit from it. They disagreed vigorously, however, over the nature of the covenant, over the nature of covenantal responsibility, and over who was counted within it. When Islam came upon the scene, it envisioned a world in which God had established covenants with many ancient communities through divine prophets. "We made a covenant with the prophets and with you [Muhammad], and Noah and Abraham and Moses and Jesus son of Mary. We made an inviolable covenant with them" (Qur'an 33:7). According to the Qur'an, God never ended those prior covenants, but every individual who failed to live up to them failed to benefit from them. Counting oneself a member of a prior covenant, therefore, did not automatically grant any special privilege in the eyes of God.

In another verse, "God made a covenant with the prophets [saying]: 'I have given you some scripture and wisdom. Then will come a prophet confirming what you have with you. Believe in him and help him.' God said: 'Do you agree to take up My covenant?' They answered, 'We agree!' He said, 'Then bear witness, and I am with you among the witnesses.' So any who turn back after this are

scoundrels" (3:81–82). This verse is understood in the interpretive
tradition to teach that Jews and Christians accepted from the truth
of their own scriptures that God would send a future prophet in
Muhammad. He would represent the best expression of monotheism, untainted by corruption and inauthentic additions. This final
covenant represented by Muhammad and the Qur'an is the most
perfect expression of God's will, but even those who count themselves within this covenantal relationship are judged by God individually based on their own personal behaviors. They cannot rely
on merit of the ancestors; they will be judged entirely on the basis
of their own lives and deeds.

The notion of original sin does not exist in Islam, so belief in
the saving power of Christ is not necessary to save yourself from
the inevitable doom that is associated in Christianity with that sin.
Similarly, while Abraham's willingness to sacrifice his own son in
response to God's command derives great merit in God's eyes, you
cannot draw on that merit to reduce any of the severity that might
be comprised in the divine decree.

The Qur'an in general does not allow intercession. "Beware of
a day when no soul can compensate for another soul, nor will intercession be accepted for it, and no ransom be received for it, nor will
they be helped" (2:48, 2:123). On the Day of Judgment, "every
soul will come pleading on its own behalf" (16:111). On the other
hand, the Qur'an says elsewhere, "All intercession is God's, who
possesses the heavens and the earth. You will be returned to Him"
(39:44). This can of course be read in more than one way. One can
gather from this that God allows intercession in certain cases, or
one can learn from this that the only intercession possible is
through God's mercy and grace.

There is no word in the Qur'an that can be translated directly
into the notion of divine grace, but God is represented repeatedly
as merciful and compassionate *(rahman* and *rahim),* and some
verses refer to God's indulgence *(fadl)* of some who deserve punishment ("If it were not for God's indulgence and mercy, you
would have been among the losers" 2:64.). We can see how the

Qur'an emphasizes that every individual will be judged on the basis of his or her own deeds, almost as if it is countering the Jewish notion of merit of the ancestors and the Christian concept of divine grace through the saving power of Christ. In Islam, God will be the sole judge. You cannot withdraw merit from the celestial bank account. You, alone, are solely accountable for your life and deeds: "Beware of a day when no soul can compensate for another, nor will intercession be accepted for it, nor will ransom be received for it" (2:48).

This position is indeed a powerful one in Islam, but it seems not to have been entirely satisfactory to all Muslims. There remained an equally powerful urge to accept the notion of intercession from the righteous, and the Qur'an was understood by some to allow this. "Who may intercede with Him except by His permission?" (2:255). "Those who pray without [God] are incapable of intercession, [all] except those who knowingly bear witness to the truth" (43:86).

As a result of this tension between the justice of individual judgment and the hope for assistance from the righteous, the one religious ancestor who came to be considered by many to be saintly enough to be worthy of providing intercession on behalf of believers is the Prophet, Muhammad. This is supported by the Hadith, a vast literature made up of short accounts of statements or behaviors of Muhammad, and the most authoritative religious literature of Islam after the Qur'an. The Hadith frequently singles out Muhammad as having been given the right of intercession on the Day of Judgment. Perhaps the most beautiful articulation of this theme, and one that is deeply aware of the notion of merit of the ancients, is the following passage in the Hadith collection compiled by Al-Bukhari in the eighth century.[6] The following was said to have occurred at an occasion when many people were gathered together at the occasion of a meal with Muhammad:

Some meat was brought before the Messenger of God. He ate some of it and then said: "I will be the head of the people on the Day of Resurrection. Do you know why? God will gather all humanity from the most ancient to the most recent on one plain so that the caller will make them able to hear his voice and the watcher will see them all. The sun will come very close, and the people will suffer such distress and trouble that they will not be able to bear it. They will say: 'Don't you see what has happened to you? Won't you look for someone who will intercede with your Lord for you?' So they will go to Adam and say, 'You are the father of humanity and God created you with His own hands. He ordered the angels to prostrate to you and taught you the names of all things; so please intercede for us with your Lord so that He may relieve us from this place of ours.' Adam will say, 'My Lord is angrier with me than ever before or after. He forbade me [from eating the fruit of] the tree, but I disobeyed Him. I am not fit for this [i.e., intercession for you]. My own soul! My own soul! Go to someone else. Go to Noah, for he was the first messenger sent by God to the people of the earth.' They will go to him and say, 'Please intercede for us with your Lord!' He will answer, 'My Great Lord is angrier with me than ever before or after. I had [been given the power to make one, single effectual] appeal in prayer, and I made it against my own people. I am not fit for this. My own soul! My own soul! Go to someone else. Go to Abraham, the Friend of God.' They will go to him and say, 'Please intercede for us with your Lord!' He will answer, 'My Lord is angrier with me than ever before or after. I told three lies![7] My own soul! My own soul! Go to someone else. Go to Moses, the servant to whom God spoke [directly] and gave the Torah.' So they will go to him and say, 'Please intercede for us with your Lord!' He will answer, 'My Lord is angrier with me than ever before or after. I killed a person who was not himself a killer. I am not fit for this. Go to Jesus, the servant of God who spoke from the cradle, His Apostle and

God's word and His spirit.' So they will go to him and say, 'Please intercede for us with your Lord!' He will answer, 'My Lord is angrier with me than ever before or after,' though he will not mention a specific sin. 'I am not fit for this. My own soul! My own soul! Go to Muhammad, the servant of God whose past and future sins were forgiven by God.' So they will come to me and I will proceed until I will ask my Lord's permission and I will be granted permission. When I see my Lord I will fall down in prostration and He will let me remain in that state as long as He wishes. Then I will be addressed. 'Raise your head. Ask, and it will be granted; say, and your saying will be heard; intercede, and your intercession will be accepted.' I will raise my head and praise God with an invocation that He will teach me. Then I will intercede. He will fix a limit for [my intercession], and I will cause them to enter Paradise. Then I will return to Him, and when I see my Lord, the same thing will occur. I will then intercede and He will fix a limit for [my inter-cession], and I will then cause them to enter Paradise. I will then return a third time, and then a fourth time and will say, 'No one remains in the Fire except those whom the [rules of the] Qur'an have detained and who must remain [there] forever.'" Abu Abdullah said: "This is referring to the statement of God [in the Qur'an], 'They will dwell therein forever.'" (16.29)

The second account from which this composite was made ends with God speaking to Muhammad: "...'O Muhammad, raise your head. Ask, and it will be granted. Intercede, and your inter-cession will be accepted.' So I will raise my head and say, 'My com-munity, O Lord! My community, O Lord!' It will be said, 'O Muhammad! Have those of your community who have no accounts against them enter the Gate [of heaven].'" This section remains true to the ambivalence in Islam toward intercession because it specifies that only those with no accounts against them may enter paradise. But even those without problematic accounts who may enter are limited to the religious community of Islam.

In one fell swoop this tradition invalidates the merit of the ancestors in Judaism and grace through the saving power of Christ in Christianity by restricting all ancestral and divinely sanctioned merit to the person of Muhammad. But like the others, it limits the beneficiaries of intercession to members of the one chosen religious community—in this case, the community of Muslims.

Despite the radical narrowing of meritorious intercession to Muhammad, Muslims have always appealed to righteous forbears to intercede on their behalf. This is especially true among the Shia branch of Islam, where it is quite acceptable to appeal for intercession from the righteous. Sunni Islam is far more reticent, but many nevertheless expect a certain benefit from the overflow of merit associated with the exceptionally righteous ancestors. Just as some Christians appeal to the saints and visit holy places in hope of deriving benefit from the association and some Jews visit the graves of holy Rabbis in hope of receiving blessing, some Muslims visit the graves and shrines of saintly religious leaders and Sufi sheiks. The notion of merit of the ancients in Islam is found in other forms in addition to visitations of saints' tombs. One is in the question of which son was intended to be the one for sacrifice in the story of Abraham.

While Jews refer to the story in Genesis 22 as the Akedah (Binding) and Christians refer to it as the Sacrifice, Muslims have their own term for it: *al-Dhabih* (the Intended Sacrifice). The story occurs in the Qur'an in chapter 37, verses 99–113. In the biblical version, it is clear that Isaac was the son chosen for sacrifice. His name is mentioned in the narrative five times, and in any case, his older brother, Ishmael, had already been sent away from the family in the previous chapter (chapter 21). There could be no question of the intended victim in the biblical story. The Qur'anic story is quite different, however. The name of Abraham's son is never uttered within the narrative, and the account of Ishmael's banishment does not occur in the Qur'an. What is more, there are no markers within the actual Qur'anic story that could be used confidently to identify either son. This seems to have troubled the early Muslim scholars and Qur'an interpreters quite a bit; of the hundreds and thousands of pages of Qur'an commentary that emerged over the centuries to respond to the story of the Intended Sacrifice, the greatest amount of material, by far, is dedicated to the question of the son's identity.

The Muslim sages were divided over which son was intended, and they engaged in deep analysis of the story from a variety of disciplines. Some of the arguments hinged on where the story took place: if in Jerusalem, it had to have been Isaac because there is no record in the Qur'an or the Bible that Isaac ever left the Holy Land. But if the near-sacrifice took place in Mecca, it had to have been Ishmael because although the Qur'an does not contain any reference to Ishmael having been cast out of the Abrahamic family, he does end up in Mecca, where he helps his father Abraham raise up the foundations of the holy Ka'ba (2:125–132). And while the Qur'an does not mention Ishmael's banishment, the legendary Islamic literature that grew up around the Qur'an does contain a story that is very similar to that found in the Bible. In the Islamic versions however, rather than having been cast out into a deserted area local to the Holy Land, Abraham personally brings Ishmael and his mother Hagar to Mecca. Today, the end of the Muslim pilgrimage festival called the Hajj commemorates the near-sacrifice of Ishmael in a large group sacrifice of thousands of animals, whose meat is distributed to the poor. But the Festival of Sacrifice, as it is known, was not always associated with Abraham's near-sacrifice of his son. It reflects a very ancient custom that may or may not have emerged as a commemoration of Ishmael having accepted his divinely commanded fate with rectitude and righteous courage.

According to most of the early Qur'an interpreters, the answer to the question of which son Abraham intended to sacrifice lies in the two sentences that end the narrative: "And We gave [Abraham] the good news of Isaac, a prophet, one of the righteous. And We blessed him and Isaac, but among their descendents are those who do good and those who clearly wrong themselves" (37:112–113). For some of the early Muslim scholars, these verses proved that Ishmael was the intended sacrifice. Since God gave Abraham the good news of Isaac at the conclusion of the narrative, he must not have even been born when the action took place. The birth of Isaac was therefore God's reward for the extraordinary integrity of Abraham and his older son. Other scholars, however, came away from these final verses with the opposite conclusion: the divine reward for Abraham and Isaac's willingness to go along without question was the divine blessing and the good news that Isaac would become a righteous prophet. According to this view, Isaac is thus personally rewarded for his fortitude in the face of the mighty trial. Which reading is the correct one? God only knows!

Although the early Muslim scholars were divided over the identity of the Intended Sacrifice, a consensus gradually emerged that it was Ishmael, based on both the biblical and the ancient Arabian genealogies. Earlier, we discussed the divide between Isaac and Ishmael in the biblical history of humanity. Although Ishmael received a divine blessing that was not insignificant, he was also mysteriously removed from the ongoing history of humanity as narrated in the Bible (Gen. 17:19–21, 21:9–21). The covenantal history of Israel moved from that generation onward through the line of Isaac, and Ishmael returned to the narrative only long enough to join his brother Isaac in burying their father Abraham (Gen. 25:9). Ishmael dropped out of biblical history, but his children did not. As the prophecy of Genesis 17 mentioned, Ishmael became the father of twelve sons, who become the heads of twelve tribes. The names of those sons are listed in Genesis 25:13–15: the firstborn was Nevayot, then Qedar, Adbe'el, Mivsam, Mishma, Dumah, Massa, Hadad, Tema, Yetur, Naphish, and Qedmah. Some of these names are unknown outside of these verses, but others have a clear historical and literary association with Arabs and Arabia.

For example, Nevayot and Qedar are referenced in Isaiah 60:66 as connected to the famous incense trade, which was an economic monopoly of Arabs in the ancient Near East. Incense was a required part of the sacrificial worship ceremonies throughout the ancient Near East, but it was grown almost entirely in southern Arabia. Arabs cultivated it from the sap of certain trees and transported it up the western coastline of Arabia northward to Gaza on the Mediterranean by camel caravan. Dumah is most likely a reference to an oasis on a parallel caravan route east of Petra in today's Jordan, called Dumat al-Jandal.

Hadad is a common Arabic name to this day, held by Jews, Christians, and Muslims alike. It is translated, literally, as "smith." Tema is associated with Arabian kings in Jeremiah 25:23–24. Yetur is associated with an ancient oasis in a region of Arabia called the Nejd. Yetur and Naphish are listed together among a confederation of enemies of the Israelites called Hagarites *(hagri'im)* in the later history of 1 Chronicles 5:10–19. These Hagarites are identified by the genealogies as being tribes organized around their ancestor, Hagar, mother of Ishmael: "And in the days of [King] Saul they made war on the Hagarites, who fell by their hand; and they dwelt in their tents throughout all the region east of Gil'ad.... The Reubenites, Gadites, and the half-tribe of Menasseh have warriors who carry shield and sword, draw the bow, and are experienced at war—44,760, ready for service. They made war on the Hagarites— Yetur, Nafish, and Nodav. They prevailed against them; the Hagarites and all who were with them were delivered into their hands, for they cried to God in battle and God responded to their entreaty because they trusted in Him."

Ishmael, therefore, is associated in the Bible with peoples who are later identified as Arabs. Many centuries afterward, he became a primary figure in Arabian history. According to ancient Arabian legends, Abraham brought Ishmael personally to Mecca, where he settled him and made sure that he would survive in the desert. The Qur'an itself testifies to this: "Remember when Abraham said, My Lord! Make this region safe and preserve me and my children from worshiping idols.... Our Lord! I have settled some of my offspring in a valley of unsown land, near Your sacred House, our Lord, that they may keep up prayers. So make the hearts of some people fond of them, and provide them with fruits, so that they may be grateful" (14:35–37). God's sacred house in this text is considered by all commentators to be in Mecca, the most sacred holy place in Islam. We have already noted that in another Qur'anic verse, Abraham and Ishmael actually raise up the foundations of the Ka'ba and build it as a sacred house of worship to the One Great God (2:125–129).

The circle is closed with the early Muslim genealogies. Like the Israelites, the Arabs were very concerned with kinship relations and with long family histories. The long genealogies of the book of Genesis in chapters 5, 10, and 11 find their parallels in early biographical histories of Muhammad. In fact, according to Islamic tradition, Muhammad descended directly from Abraham's son Ishmael. With this in mind, it should not be surprising that Muslims would be inclined to consider the unnamed son of the Qur'anic version of the Intended Sacrifice to have been Ishmael rather than Isaac. This is articulated in a number of traditions and interpretations. One of particular interest was articulated by the famous thirteenth-century Muslim scholar and Qur'an interpreter, Ismail Ibn Kathir, who cited a tradition in which the great caliph 'Umar Ibn 'Abd al-'Aziz was asked who he considered to be the son referenced anonymously in Qur'an 37:

> 'Umar said to him: "I would never have considered that issue before...." Then he sent for a man who was with him in Syria. He was a Jew who had converted to Islam and had become a good Muslim. It became apparent that he had been one of the religious scholars of the Jews [before his conversion], so 'Umar b. 'Abd al-'Aziz decided to ask him about it. Muhammad b. Ka'b al-Qurazi said: "I was with 'Umar b. 'Abd al-'Aziz when he said: 'Which of Abraham's two sons was he commanded to sacrifice?' [The previously Jewish convert] answered: Ishmael. And by God, O Caliph, the Jews know that. However, they envy the Arab community because their father was the one commanded [to be sac-

rificed] and he is the one who is ascribed for merit for his steadfastness. But they deny that and claim that it was Isaac because Isaac was their father.'"[8]

Which opinion is correct? It is actually impossible to know. It appears that the Qur'an purposefully refrained from providing the name of the son in order to stress the more important existential messages embedded in the passage. Recall that the Qur'an emphasizes the importance of each individual's responsibility for his or her behavior. Merit of the ancestors and divine grace through the saving power of Jesus are not considered acceptable means for avoiding the divine decree in the Qur'an. The Qur'an emphasizes individual responsibility. There is always the possibility that God may forgive according to his mercy and compassion, but that divine mercy cannot be relied upon. This position is both noble and ethical, but difficult to accept for the reason with which we began this chapter. Most of us are well aware of our innermost weaknesses, and we are anxious about what that may mean for our future in this world and the next. In the next layer of Islamic religious literature, therefore, it was understood that at the very least, the righteous and saintly prophet Muhammad would intercede on behalf of his religious community. And Muhammad's intercession is efficacious, according to the Hadith, while the pious merit of all the other biblical ancients, including Abraham and Jesus, is found lacking.

This position is an expression of the polemic associated with chosenness and the tension in all three religions between theologies of personal responsibility and theologies of saintly intercession. On the one hand, we are all individually responsible to act ethically, despite our human weaknesses and our tendency to fail to do the right thing. On the other hand, all three religions claim a unique and chosen association with God in which its own prophets and saints have a special relationship with God that benefits the religious community that they represent. There is, therefore, help for the believers in each system, but only the insiders in each may benefit from it. But which system represents the divine truth? Who among the prophets and messianic figures is the most authentic? Which prophets and heroes can truly intercede on behalf of the religious community that they represent? Who, therefore, truly benefits from the merit and intercession of the ancients?

The answer to these questions depends, of course, on who is speaking. Each monotheistic system claims exclusive benefits and excludes the others. Unfortunately, the argument is not only theological. In certain periods of history, it is argued through politics, violence, and even war.

8

The Legacy of Chosenness

We noted above how the sense of exclusive relationship with God came to be experienced by some believers as a social truth, as an existential value that placed them in a category above the rest of humanity. This sense of exclusivity was articulated in a variety of ways. Sometimes it appeared almost racial in its tone, sometimes xenophobic. It was sometimes expressed in terms of mission, at other times, as crusade. Some believers read signs in the stars or in history to prove that they were more worthy than nonbelievers. Although the early followers of every monotheistic movement suffered for their loyalty and faith in their religion during the period of its emergence, in later periods too many became willing to bring suffering on those who might dare to challenge their faith. In the following we will observe how this reversal became realized in history. Every case was influenced by the particularities and specifics of the historical situation.

Ancient Israel: Separation for Preservation

We have noted how the hierarchy between believers and nonbelievers is most obvious in the Hebrew Bible: "Of all the peoples on earth the Lord your God chose you to be His treasured people"

(Deut. 7:6–8, cf. 14:2). "You shall be holy to Me, for I the Lord am holy, and I have set you apart from other peoples to be Mine" (Lev. 20:26). These verses convey a combination of elitism and separatism. They reflect the historical context of the ancient Near East, where all religions were ethnically organized and defined. Similar to their neighboring polytheistic communities, when Israel's god was conceived simply as the "god of Israel" it was natural and logical to consider the bond with God unique and exclusive.

But as biblical scholars now tend to agree, the limited "god of Israel" transformed in the eyes of the Israelites to become the One Great God of the entire universe. This happened roughly around the time of the destruction of the First Temple and the period of the later prophets in the sixth century BCE. The notion of many gods, each with an exclusive relationship with its own religious people, was natural in a polytheistic world. But the divine chosenness of a single ethnic group that would be so natural in a world of ethnic polytheism seems to have become problematic to the universal perspective of monotheism. Some biblical texts reflect that ambivalence. Exodus 19:5, for example, makes the special relationship conditional on the Israelites properly observing their covenantal obligations. The prophet Amos expressed a great deal of discomfort with covenantal exclusivism when he recited: "To Me, O Israelites, you are just like the Ethiopians, declares the Lord. True, I brought Israel up from the land of Egypt, but also the Philistines from Caphtor and the Arameans from Kir" (Amos 9:7). The exclusive, chosen relationship between God and Israel becomes a literary vehicle for God to chastise his own people: "You alone have I singled out of all the families of the earth. That is why I will call you to account for all your iniquities" (Amos 3:2).

Remember that people worshiped according to their ethnic or national identity in the ancient Near East. The notion of religious conversion was not a conceptual possibility at the time. Even after the transition to monotheism, proselytism was literally inconceivable. It seemed impossible to imagine withdrawing your allegiance to a personal tribal or national god and then giving it to another that represented a different ethno-religious community. Not surprisingly, therefore, there is no evidence of Israelites attempting to recruit non-Israelites to their ranks. The relationship of ancient Israel to other nations was never one of mission, and there is no reference to proselytizing in the Hebrew Bible. This fact is in stark contrast with the New Testament, for example (see Matt. 28:18–20, Acts 10, 15) or the Qur'an ("Invite [all] to the way of your Lord with wisdom and beautiful preaching; and argue with them in ways that are best and most gracious: For your Lord knows best who has strayed from His Path, and who receives guidance" 16:125.). Rabbinic Judaism also includes the acceptance of proselytes (Talmud, Yebamot 47a; Kiddushin 67a–b, 73a). Not only was proselytizing foreign to the world of the Hebrew Bible, but even accepting a *voluntary* proselyte was so rare that an entire biblical book was composed around this unusual theme: the book of Ruth.

The lack of reference to mission in the Hebrew Bible may have also been related to the lack of a developed notion of reward and punishment in an afterlife. The notion of an afterlife is simply not a theme of the Hebrew Bible. It seems to have found its way only into the very last layers of biblical literature through influence from Babylonia, to which the Judeans were exiled after the destruction of the First Temple in Jerusalem. Modern readers tend to presume that heaven and hell are a core part of the Hebrew Bible, but this is simply not the case. The word *shamayim* (heaven) is a reference to the sky or to the abode of God. It was not a place where humans could enter after death in this world.[1] The notions of a heavenly hereafter and a place of hellish doom seem to have emerged only in the period of Late Antiquity, after the biblical period. In the Hebrew Bible, all reward and punishment was believed to have been meted out by God in this world (Leviticus 26; Deuteronomy 28). God's salvation was neither a revival of the dead nor an eternity in otherworldly misery or bliss. It was, rather, a future time when peace would reign on earth (Isa. 2:1–4; Mic. 4:1–5), and certainly not salvation from the pains of hell. In the Hebrew Bible, references to redemption are to redemption from slavery, not redemption from hellfire. Only in the very last chapter of the most recent biblical book, the book of Daniel, is there a reference that seems to reflect a clear belief in resurrection, judgment, and eternal existence in a world outside of our own. But even there (Dan. 12:1–3), only the righteous are rewarded. There is no mention of the wicked suffering punishment in an afterlife or another world.[2] Without such a notion, it would have been a conceptual impossibility to "save souls" through a program of mission.

In the early layers of the Bible, the Israelites interacted quite easily and often with their non-Israelite neighbors. Great heroes of the Bible such as Joseph and Moses even married daughters of polytheistic priests (Gen. 41:45; Exod. 2:15–21). As the Israelites became more fully dedicated to monotheism, however, they found that they needed to separate from their polytheistic neighbors. It became ever more important to separate from the religious practices of neighboring peoples who worshiped limited gods and powers. It is likely that a number of social practices that emerged in the Bible, such as strict dietary laws, did so, at least in part, in order to separate Israelites from social interaction with other peoples. The religion of the Bible certainly would not have placed such an emphasis on separation if it had been interested in mission.

We noted earlier that the only way to leave your ancestral religion in the ancient Near East was to assimilate into another ethnic group or nation. If your social and ritual practice required behaviors that discouraged social interaction with other peoples, the members of your community would be much less likely to become known and thus perhaps become attractive to them. Intermarriage is always a threat to the unity and survival of a small community, and the biblical Israelites and, later, the Jews faced this challenge for most of their history. Even those biblical nations such as the Egyptians and Edomites, whom scripture permitted Israelites to marry, had to live at least three generations among the Israelites before they were acceptable marriage partners (Deut. 23:8–9). During that time they would have assimilated into the Israelite culture and religious system.

These kinds of rules and behavioral expectations do not reflect political power. The Israelites never really achieved great political dominance. Even during the greatest period of national power, under Kings David and Solomon (which only lasted eighty years), the nation was always threatened by foreign powers such as Egypt and Mesopotamian civilizations that were more powerful and often on the march. As the historian David Biale has so aptly written, "For most of the time from the beginning of the Israelite settlement in the land of Canaan to the fall of the Second Temple, the Jewish people lived in the shadow of great empires, rarely enjoying what would today be called full national sovereignty."[3] The elitism of Israelite monotheism, therefore, and its sense of chosenness, ironically remained the trait of a small and often embattled community. Israelite chosenness included no theology or political ideology of mission or conversion, and it generally left others to practice whatever religion they wished as long as it did not impact negatively on the religious or political independence of Israel.

There was one exceptional instance, however, in which the religion of Israel was forcibly imposed upon another community. This was the case of the conversion of the Idumeans under the Judean ruler, John Hyrcanus, in the second century BCE. This occurred after Hellenism had entered the Near East, and the exceptional action was possible only because of a confluence of factors: the influence of Hellenism with its notion of conversion, the temporary vacuum of Greek political power in the area, and the sudden rise to power of a Jewish kingdom led by priest-kings called the Hasmoneans. The episode represents the first known case where monotheism was imposed on nonbelievers en masse. We know little about the program or the process, but the Idumeans seem to have integrated fairly well into the Hasmonean kingdom (a phenomenon that would find subsequent historical parallels with mass conversions of polytheists to other forms of monotheism). Many upper-class Idumeans moved into key social and governmental positions in the Jewish state of Judea. This exception proved the general rule:

the Israelite sense of chosenness was elitist but disinterested. It felt no compulsion to require others to realize the truth of its own religious system. The obligation of biblical Israel was limited to living according to God's will. It required no mission to recruit others who might worship other gods.

Rabbinic Judaism: Chosenness and Consolation

Rabbinic Judaism began to emerge during the late Second Temple period. This was after the notions of conversion, mission, and salvation in a world to come had entered the biblical world through the influence of Hellenism and Babylonian and Persian traditions. Rabbinic Judaism emerged into history during an extended period of Jewish political powerlessness. With the destruction of the Second Temple in 70 CE, Jewish communities lived in political exile under governments ruled by non-Jews, even in the land of Israel. There were two important stages in this period of emergent rabbinic Judaism.

In the first, from the first century BCE to the beginning of the fourth century CE, the Roman Empire was pagan. Although the empire was ascendant, Roman paganism was not, and many Greco-Romans were in search of a religion that was more meaningful than the traditional one based on the increasingly irrelevant polytheistic pantheon of squabbling gods. We noted above how a variety of new religious movements in addition to rabbinic Judaism and Christianity began emerging at this time. They are sometimes called "mystery cults," such as Eleusinian mysteries, Mithraic mysteries (or Mithraism), and Orphic mysteries. Many Romans tried out these new religions during this time, and many also observed Jews engaging in their own religious practice. Not a few became interested in Judaism and began experimenting with Jewish practices that brought them into the orbit of the Jewish communities of the Holy Land and in other parts of the Roman world. These practices included at least partial observance of Jewish dietary laws, ritual worship, study, and even circumcision among men. By this time in the postbiblical period of Greco-Roman antiquity, the notion of conversion had entered the Near East. It had become possible for non-Jews to enter into the community of Israel as converts.

Emerging rabbinic Judaism became popular among the Greco-Romans, and so many entered into Judaism that historians estimate some 10 percent of the entire Roman Empire was Jewish by the first century CE. In the eastern region comprising today's Israel/Palestine, Jordan, Lebanon, and Syria, some 20 percent of the total population were Jews. During this period, a sense of mission, or at least a far greater willingness to accept proselytes than in the biblical period, developed among some Jews. This was probably influenced by the competition resulting from the early Christian claim that Christianity had replaced the old religion of the Bible as the "true Israel" *(verus Israel),* a newly chosen people who had chosen Jesus as their Messiah.

Rabbinic Jews, who represented the monotheistic religious establishment at the time, felt threatened by the emerging competition and the Christian claims to exclusivity. The New Testament records that some Jews harassed the early Christians and tried to prevent the new movement from succeeding. But both Jews and Christians were living under the rule of pagan Rome at the time, which had little institutional love for either system. Both sides tried to mobilize their members to gain influence and increase their followers, but it was impossible to go beyond the powers of personal persuasion to do so. Political or military power could not possibly be employed to expand the influence of either community, because all power lay with the Romans.

In the second stage of emerging rabbinic Judaism, the Roman Empire had Christianized. This occurred in the fourth century, under Constantine, with the result that Christianity absorbed and took on the power and influence of the empire. When the establishment religion of Rome became Christianity, the old paganism was outlawed, but Judaism kept its status as a tolerated minority tradition. That tolerated status soon eroded. Jews were immediately forbidden from proselytizing and from marrying Christians. They were also forbidden certain economic rights by law and were prohibited from building synagogues. In crude terms, Christianity had won the competition for the prize of the empire. Judaism had lost, and that loss was not merely spiritual. It had severe economic, political, and social consequences. In this environment, the old monotheistic sense of chosenness and elitism among Jews did not weaken, but it tended to become internalized, partly as a consolation for lack of outward religious and political success.

Under Byzantine Christian law, mission by Jews became a capital crime. If anything, then, rabbinic Judaism separated itself increasingly from Gentiles. But this does not represent a withdrawal from intellectual engagement with non-Jews. In fact, as Christian writers from this period convey, a nagging articulation of Jewish superiority continued to plague many Christian thinkers. The fourth-century church father St. John Chrysostom opined the attraction of Judaism to new Christians in the capital city of Constantinople, despite the legal restrictions against the Jews. The old Jewish sense of chosenness and its attendant elitism seems not to have declined much at the time. However, that sense of Jewish religious superiority could not be applied to political, social, or military policy.

This, then, became the legacy of Judaism. It has never been much of a proselytizing religion, and, aside from the brief episode with the Idumeans, it has never harnessed the apparatus of state to promote its religious agenda.[4] The reason for this is probably as simple as it is structural. Between the time of the Bible to the establishment of the state of Israel, Judaism was never a religion of a state that could apply its sense of chosenness elitism to public policy. Jewish proselytizing was suppressed in the Christian world, and when it also became a capital crime in the Muslim world it became virtually impossible anywhere. As a result, perhaps, some of those energies associated with chosenness elitism became sublimated and applied to other pursuits. Chosenness became largely a form of consolation among Jews.

Christianity and Islam: Religions of Empire

We have seen how Christianity emerged in the same general environment of political powerlessness under Roman rule as rabbinic Judaism. In fact, Christians held less power and were held with far more disdain by Rome than Jews for most of the period from the days of Jesus to the Christianization of the empire. After the end of the Jewish uprisings against Rome in the middle of the second century, Christians were persecuted physically by the Romans more than the Jews were. But despite the attraction that Judaism represented for many Romans, Christianity had greater success in making inroads among Greco-Romans seeking a new faith system. It became more successful in attracting followers than all the other religious options of the Greco-Roman world.

By the middle of the fourth century, Christians found themselves the dominant and then ruling religion of the empire. For the first time in human history, monotheists controlled a world empire with all of its institutions of power: political rule, administrative bureaucracies, tax collection, control of the media and education, and the military. This was the first opportunity to apply the religious ideology of monotheist elitism to imperial law, and it began to be done early on. Before the end of the century, pagan practices were outlawed, and even many monotheistic practices that were not in line with the practices of the Christians in power were prohibited or restricted. Aside from the brief Idumean episode, this was the first time that monotheism was forcibly imposed. The religion of Christianity became a mover of imperial Roman diplomacy. It was the first time in human history that the forceful imposition of monotheism became a governmental policy.

The Hellenistic notion of conversion was not the reason for the change. After all, by the fourth century, proselytizing had been an option for Jews and Christians for hundreds of years. The real motivation for the policy of forced imposition of the religion of the "chosen" was simply that it was possible. When Christians made the transition from persecuted people to people in power, it became all too easy for some to simply reverse the policies that had been leveled against them. Christianity became the state religion. When that occurred, not only were all forms of polytheism outlawed, but even the practice of Christianity became a crime if it did not conform to the type of Christianity established as orthodoxy by the rulers of the empire.

When monotheism became the religion of the empire through the Christianization of Rome, it naturally took on an imperialist worldview. This is ironic, considering that Christianity originated as a persecuted religious minority that struggled to survive in the face of the overwhelming power of a violently unsympathetic empire. On the other hand, it is not illogical. Christian thinkers of the time wrote that history had proven the divinely chosen status of Christianity and the church. A great church historian who lived through the Christianization of the Roman Empire, Eusebius of Caesaria, was one of them. Eusebius was the bishop of Caesaria in Roman Palestine and also the personal biographer of Emperor Constantine, who legalized Christianity in the empire. In Constantine's biography, Eusebius wrote, "But now, that liberty is restored, and that serpent driven from the administration of public affairs by the providence of the Supreme God, and our instrumentality, we trust that all can see the efficacy of the Divine power, and that they who through fear of persecution or through unbelief have fallen into any errors, will now acknowledge the true God, and adopt in future that course of life which is according to truth and rectitude" (*Life of Constantine* 2:46).

For Eusebius and other church leaders and theologians, the Christianization of the most powerful empire on earth was nothing less than a divine sign confirming God's preference for the truth of Christianity. After having gained the reigns of imperial power, then, Christianity became an imperialist religion itself. The imperial codes of the Christian Roman emperors during the earliest period of Christian control, from Theodosius and Justinian onward, applied the power of the state to enforce religious ideology and practice throughout the empire.

A similar phenomenon occurred when Islam became the religion of empire. Like all new religious movements, Islam emerged as a minority faction and was opposed by the establishments that found it threatening. It nevertheless managed to prevail over persecution. Eventually it became the established religion of the great Muslim empire, or caliphate, led by a ruler called a caliph. As in the case of Christianity, the elitist ideology of monotheism combined with governmental power to create an imperial interpretation of religion that imposed its religious ideology by the power of the state. In the case of Christianity, the mechanism was the imperial codes mentioned above. The centralized nature of Christianity's legal codes reflects the culture and organization of the early church. Islam was always less centralized than Christianity. More akin to Judaism in this regard, Islam has no central religious figures such as bishops, patriarchs, or popes. Rather than through a centralized caliphal decree, therefore, the political imposition of religious law and rule was developed and authorized by Muslim religious scholars in a legal system called shari'a. Because of Islam's quick political domination of the Near East very early on in its process of emergence, Islamic religious law had no time to develop until after Islam had become an imperial religion. The general attitude of the shari'a toward non-Muslims, therefore, tends to express an imperial worldview. It is in the main universal, triumphant, and reflective of a point of view shaped by the power of empire.

It must be clarified here that not all expressions of Islam or Christianity are imperialist. Both religions include powerful and influential schools of thought that do not seek to dominate or impose their religious power or ideologies on nonbelievers. Some of these developed before the religious leadership became the rulers of empire, and some developed as countermovements that opposed the natural tendency of powerful religious bureaucracies toward religious imperialism. But because those in power had the resources and political support to promote their religious interpretations, they have tended to dominate, so that many religious sources may be found in both Christianity and Islam to support or promote religious imperialism.

There is a major difference, however, between the imperialism of Islam and that of Christianity. That difference seems to be based on the particular history of each in its transition from opposition (or persecuted) religion to religion of state. As Christianity emerged into history in the first century, it found itself in intense competition with one established religious community (rabbinic Judaism). Both claimed that only it represented the true will of the universal God. As Islam emerged into history in the seventh century, however, it found itself competing with a number of established expressions of monotheism and some new forms of Arabian monotheism as well (one rival form of Arabian monotheism was even headed by a man named Musaylima, a variation of the name Muslim). In the Arabian historical context of the seventh century, therefore, there were many monotheisms, each claiming the unique status of being the chosen of God.

To recap our history of monotheisms for a moment, recall that in the very earliest period, when only one expression of monotheism existed, it was perceived by the community of monotheists to be the one chosen community in covenantal relationship with the One Great God. This was Israelite monotheism, struggling to survive in a world of ancient Near Eastern polytheism. The story of this struggle is recorded in the texts of the Hebrew Bible. Israelite monotheism never remained static. Its development can be traced in the Bible itself, and it continued to evolve, with the majority of Israel eventually transforming into adherents of rabbinic Judaism around the same time that Christianity was born. When two discreet expressions of monotheism existed side-by-side, the status of chosenness was considered by both communities to be a zero-sum equation, and this perspective is reflected in both the New Testament and the Talmud.

Islam emerged centuries later and in a world in which there were a variety of competing expressions of monotheism. Not only were there the religious orthodoxies of Judaism and Christianity, but there were also unorthodox representations of each, and some of these had a lot of followers. A number of these had made their way into the Arabian peninsula by the seventh century, and each one claimed to hold the proper understanding and response to the divine will. There is also evidence of other expressions of monotheism at the time that were neither Jewish nor Christian, including indigenous Arabian expressions of monotheism or proto-monotheism. To the early Muslims, therefore, it was not natural to conceive of chosenness as a zero-sum equation. The many expressions of monotheism contemporary to emerging Islam prevented an absolutist perspective from becoming dominant among early Muslims.

The Qur'an represents the earliest layers of Islamic thought and captures the religious perspective of the early Muslim community. It mentions a number of times that any expression of monotheism merits the world to come. We cited this important verse above: "Those who believe, and who are Jews, and Christians and Sabaeans—whoever believes in God and the Last Day and who work righteousness—they have their reward with their Lord, they shall not fear nor should they grieve" (2:62, 5:69, 22:17). There are counterarguments in the Qur'an as well, which condemn Jews and Christians for not accepting the prophethood of Muhammad. But the openness of the Qur'an toward other expressions of monotheism cannot be denied. This is not the case with early Christianity. The notion of salvation in the New Testament is repeatedly restricted to those who accept belief in the saving power of Christ (John 3:36, 15:5–6; Acts 4:12). All were invited, but those who could or would not accept belief in salvation through Christ were excluded.

Both the New Testament and the Qur'an were strongly influenced by the nature of the environments of their birth. The Qur'an is less exclusive than the New Testament in its view of other monotheisms simply because of the multi-monotheistic environment out of which it emerged. Ironically, perhaps, these same monotheistic communities ended up opposing the newly emerging Muslim community. The major existential threat to the Muslims represented in the Qur'an, however, is Arabian polytheism.

Like Christianity, Islam became the religion of empire, and for both religions, the needs, desires, and greed of empire made some radical changes in the articulation of the religion under its influence. In Christianity, the overwhelming emphasis on the suffering of the weak in the New Testament, for example, was often overruled by the interests of the powerful leaders of the empire. In Islam, the inclusiveness of the Qur'an was often overruled by the exclusive outlook of the rulers of the caliphate. And in both cases, the elitism of chosenness in its own brand of monotheism became realized through the law and politics of power. When they became imperial religions, they privileged their own forms of monotheism through imperial law.

One important difference must be noted about this legal partiality. Under the caliphate, Jews and Christians held second-class status that in some periods and places resulted in persecution and even massacres, but Christianity and Judaism always remained legal religions. Jews and Christians were free to practice their religion without interference. They were protected by law according to the shari'a.

In Christianity, however, contrary forms of monotheistic practice were eventually outlawed completely. Heresy was punishable by death in both Christianity and Islam, but under the Christian imperial system, Islam was, to most religious thinkers, not considered worthy of consideration as a religion. The Catholic Church only recognized it fully in the 1960s under the great reforms of Vatican II. Even Judaism, which we noted above had been grandfathered into legal standing by the pagan Roman Empire, eventually lost its legal status under Christian rulers. It was preserved from destruction by the theology of Augustine and others only because it represented a degraded form of monotheism that could still be observed among humiliated Jews, and to which Christians should not belong. The degradation of the Jews in real time thus became a way of publicly demonstrating the truth of Christianity. The Jews of Christendom were protected also by the role assigned to them by Augustine at the End of Days, when it was believed that they would inevitably witness the truth of Jesus as Christ with their conversion to Christianity. Jews eventually lost their legal rights within the Christian world altogether as a result of the trend within the Church toward absolute religious totalitarianism. This remained basic policy of the Church until the Reformation forced a reevaluation of totalistic traditional imperial views.

Using a word such as "totalitarianism" is harsh to describe the absolutist position that developed within Christianity. The term was actually coined in the 1920s in reference to Italian fascism, so we naturally associate it with secular dictatorships and tyranny. This is a far cry from Christianity's historical role of caring and compassion and service to the poor and underprivileged, whether Christian or not. But the two are not mutually exclusive.

Christianity is clearly not inherently totalitarian. There was always a school of thought in Christianity, sometimes referred to as "universal reconciliation," according to which the suffering and crucifixion of Jesus provides reconciliation for all humankind, whether or not they are believers in the saving power of Christ. But this position weakened and eventually virtually disappeared after the Christianization of the Roman Empire. The dominant position of the Church then became expressed classically by the famous theological dictum, *extra Ecclesiam nulla salus* (no salvation outside the Church). This was first formulated by Cyprian of Carthage (d. 258), and was reiterated repeatedly by great popes such as Gregory the Great (d. 604), Innocent III (d. 1208), Boniface VIII (d. 1302), and authoritative Church statements such as the Fourth Lateran Council (1215) and the Council of Florence (1442). It seems clear that a strict teaching of *extra Ecclesiam nulla salus* was the dominant position among premodern Church leaders.

The quality of religious imperialism is therefore different in Christianity than in Islam, and that difference seems to have been generated significantly by the particular historical contexts out of which the two religions emerged into history. Christianity has tended toward religious totalitarianism that stressed the requirement of membership in the Church for salvation, and it is only in the last half century that progressive forces have pushed hard to try to reverse this trend. Islam does not include such a totalitarian tradition, for the Qur'an expresses repeatedly that all righteous monotheists need not fear a future salvation.

But in a surprising reversal of the modern Christian trend toward inclusion, there is a certain movement among some radical politicized Muslims toward religious totalitarianism. This trend is not based on the Qur'an, which we have observed contains repeated statements of inclusion, at least for other monotheists. The religious totalitarianism that has recently been articulated by radical, militant Muslims is an innovation that has no basis in the authority of divine scripture.

9
Does Redemption
Require Election?

The word *redemption* comes from the Latin *redemptionem,* meaning "a buying back, releasing, ransoming." It means, literally, liberation by payment of a price or ransom. Just as one can redeem a debt by paying it off or redeem a slave by buying his or her freedom, the religious meaning of redemption has a sense of ransoming from the inevitable bondage that results from sin.

This is not a neutral definition; it is a Christian definition. Jews, Muslims, Hindus, and Buddhists also have notions of redemption in their religious traditions and literatures, but their versions do not work out exactly the same way as the classical Christian perspective, for reasons that we will examine below. English speakers sometimes have difficulty understanding these kinds of religious differences because the English language has become Christianized over the centuries during which Christianity has become literally or virtually the national religion of English speakers. Because we formulate our complex thinking in language, the nature of the language we speak tends to influence our way of thinking and perceiving the world around us. You may have associates and friends fluent in English whose native tongues are Chinese or Japanese or Hindi, and you may find an occasional slight miscommunication. Yet they are fluent in English. The reason may be, simply, that the two languages' subtle meanings for key terms or concepts are different enough to cause a "disconnect" in language. It may not be big enough to even notice explicitly, but in some cases may cause some real consternation or even a barrier for deep friendship.

As I indicated at the very beginning of this book, I find Webster's 1828 *Dictionary of the English Language* particularly interesting because its American definitions are often so unabashedly Christian and its examples drawn from biblical sources. For a definition of redemption, Webster writes, "The purchase of God's favor by the death and sufferings of Christ; the ransom or deliverance of sinners from the bondage of sin and the penalties of God's violated law by the atonement of Christ. 'In whom we have redemption through his blood.' Eph. 1:7." The full passage of the King James Version of the Bible from which Webster quotes is, "In whom we have redemption through his blood, the forgiveness of sins, according to the riches of his grace. Wherein he hath abounded toward us in all wisdom and prudence" (Eph. 1:7–8). The more contemporary *Oxford Study Bible* translation reads, "In Christ our release is secured and our sins forgiven through the shedding of his blood. In the richness of his grace, God has lavished on us all wisdom and insight." Webster's *Dictionary* does not define the meaning of redemption in either Judaism or Islam.

Redemption has an English parallel in the word *salvation,* which also comes from the Latin. *Salvationem* is a noun of action deriving from *salvare,* "to save." Our English word comes from the church Latin translation of the Greek, *soteria,* related to the Greek word *soter,* meaning "savior." Based on this word is an English term that is used to describe theologies of salvation: *soteriology.* As in the definition of redemption, Webster's definition of salvation has a strong Christian influence and does not define the meaning in Judaism or Islam: "The redemption of man from the bondage of sin and liability to eternal death, and the conferring on him everlasting happiness. This is the great salvation."

The Hebrew Bible: God as Redeemer

Words that convey something like the English *redemption* and *salvation* also occur in biblical Hebrew, though the sense of saving from death or from sin is not operative there because the Christian notion of original sin is not found there directly. A Hebrew term that is usually translated into English as "salvation" is the word *yeshu'a,* but that word describes the deliverance of the Israelites from the Egyptians (Exod. 14:13) and of deliverance generally from evil or danger. Two words for redemption are used in the Hebrew Bible, constructed from the verbs *podeh* and *go'el.* As in the origin of the Latin parallels, their meanings are derived from ordinary human affairs. *Podeh* refers to paying for something to be released from the possession of one person and secured in the possession of another. It is a simple transaction in which ownership is transferred from one party to another. The person who carries out the transaction is called the *podeh.* Anyone can be a *podeh.*

The same word takes on ritual significance because of the rule in the Bible that all the firstborn, whether animal or human, belong to God. Some of these firstborn can be redeemed with a payment, and all firstborn humans (who in theory belong to God) must be redeemed as well (Exod. 13:1–2; Num. 18:15). To this day there is a ritual ceremony among some Jews based on this requirement called *pidyon haben* or "redemption of the [firstborn] son." The ritual takes place on the thirty-first day after birth, based on Numbers 15:16, and it is a simple one during which certain blessings are recited and five silver dollars (or other currency) are given to a Cohen, a male whose lineage derives from the ancient priestly families.

The word *go'el* is similar, but is used in the Bible in the context of kinship responsibility. The *go'el* is the male next of kin who takes special responsibility in the clan to protect clan property, support widows or orphans, and redeem family members who have been reduced to slavery through poverty. "If your kinsman is in straits and has to sell part of his holdings, his nearest [relative acting as] redeemer *(go'el)* shall come and redeem what his kins-man has sold" (Lev. 24:25).

In the Bible God is both *podeh* and *go'el*. The classic case of God as *podeh* is the divine redemption of the Israelites from the slavery of Egypt. "Remember that you were slaves in the land of Egypt and the Lord your God redeemed you" (Deut. 15:15). But God also delivers individuals from worldly adversity, as in 2 Samuel 4:9 and 2 Kings 1:29, where David acknowledges God's role in redeeming him from all his adversities.[1]

The other word, *go'el,* is common in the biblical prophetic writings and Psalms to convey the intimate relationship between God and his people. The word conveys the sense of family, almost as if God and Israel are together in the same family and God is the loving and responsible head of the tribe. The prophet Isaiah recites the following words of God within his prophecies of comfort, "Fear not, O [little] worm Jacob, O men of Israel, I will help you, declares the Lord, your Redeemer *(go'el),* the Holy One of Israel" (Isa. 41:14). "Thus says the Lord, the King of Israel, their Redeemer *(go'el),* the Lord of Hosts, I am the first and I am the last, and there is no god but Me" (Isa. 44:4). God is the redeemer of the orphan (Prov. 23:10–11) and of the persecuted (Job 23:25).

We need to keep in mind in our consideration of the Hebrew Bible that the notions of life after death or eternal salvation were not operative in ancient Israel, aside from the very end of the period represented by the end of the book of Daniel. We have noted above that in Hebrew scripture God rewards and punishes on this earth rather than in a future world. The teachings about divine reward and punishment are articulated in group terms. Our modern insistence on the rights and needs of the individual, sometimes even at the expense of the community, is not shared exactly in the Bible. It is true that individuals must be judged by the community for their own personal behaviors (Deut. 24:16), but the welfare of the community as a whole is determined in cosmic terms by its group behavior. Individual behaviors are judged by God as they are represented by the actions and conduct of the community as a whole.

This requires that the individual take personal responsibility for the behavior of the group. The result is that the community of Israel as a whole is rewarded or punished.

This system is commendable ethically because it requires that individuals take full responsibility for the behaviors of the group. The problem with the system is that it seems impossible for the community as a whole to ever avoid divine retribution. No matter how much we try to behave ethically as a community, there will always be some individuals who will torpedo our best efforts. Israel, therefore, often found itself punished with plague or conquest by foreign peoples, dispersed among the nations, downtrodden and unhappy. This unfortunate situation was considered to be God's will, of course. It was also considered to be cleansing and purifying. The result was that a theology emerged in the Hebrew Bible teaching that a righteous remnant of the nation of Israel that remained true to the aspirations of monotheism would be redeemed, and along with it, the remainder of the world.

Biblical notions of redemption, therefore, are for a future time on earth when life will be happy and peaceful for the community: hunger will no longer exist, bloodshed within the community will end, and wars with other communities will cease. It is a time when everyone will "sit under their own vine and fig tree, with nothing to fear" (Mic. 4:4), and it will happen in this world rather than in any world to come. There are many references to this future redemption, but the classic passage referring to such a future is Isaiah 65:17–25:

> For behold! I am creating a new heaven and a new earth. The former things shall not be remembered. They shall never come to mind. Be glad, then, and rejoice forever in what I am creating, for I shall create Jerusalem as a joy, and her people as a delight. And I will rejoice in Jerusalem and delight in her people. Never again shall be heard there the sounds of weeping and wailing. No more shall there be an infant or graybeard who does not live out his days. He who

dies at a hundred years shall be reckoned a youth, and he who fails to reach a hundred shall be reckoned accursed. They shall build houses and dwell in them. They shall plant vineyards and enjoy their fruit. They shall not build for others to dwell in, or plan for others to enjoy. For the days of My people shall be as long as the days of a tree, My chosen ones shall outlive the work of their hands. They shall not toil without purpose; they shall not bear children for terror, but they shall be a people blessed by the Lord and their offspring shall remain with them. Before they pray, I will answer. While they are still speaking, I will respond. The wolf and the lamb shall graze together, and the lion shall eat straw like the ox, and the serpent's food shall be earth. In all My sacred mount nothing evil or vile shall be done.

This moving aspiration for a future earthly redemption is articulated first and foremost in terms of the nation of Israel. This should not be surprising, given the national nature of religion in the ancient Near East and the fact that only Israel was truly monotheistic at that time. The future is articulated in reference to the past, so in the Hebrew Bible there is great aspiration for a time in which God will bring a final and great redemption for Israel, just as God redeemed the Israelites from Egyptian slavery. "Assuredly, a time is coming—declares the Lord—when it shall no more be said, 'As the Lord lives, who brought the Israelites out of the land of Egypt,' but rather, 'As the Lord lives, who brought out and led the offspring of the House of Israel from the northland and from all the lands to which I have banished them.' And they shall dwell upon their own soil" (Jer. 23:7–8).

Just as the redemption from Egypt was wrought through violence and destruction of Israel's Egyptian enemy, so too will the final redemption include the destruction of Israel's current and future enemies. The references are many and they are not all consistent, but the general thrust is clear: Israel's enemies will be crushed while Israel will be restored to its privileged state. In the final redemption at the End of Days, the Children of Israel will be gathered together from the four corners of the earth (Isa. 11:12), the redeemed Israelites will experience everlasting joy (Isa. 51:11), the kings of the nations will come to realize that they erred in their brutal treatment of Israel (Isa. 52:13–53:5), the Jerusalem Temple will be rebuilt (Ezek. 40), the ruined cities of Israel will be restored (Ezek. 16:55), and all Israel will know God's teachings (Jer. 31:33).

Although the joy and happiness of God's redemption is centered on the one community of believers that recognizes the One Great God, the entire world will also benefit. The false idols worshiped by the nations will disappear and only the One Great God will be worshiped (Isa. 2:17–18)—remember that these texts emerged before any other forms of monotheism existed—evil and tyranny will be overcome (Isa. 11:4), weapons of war will be destroyed (Ezek. 39:9), the many nations will voluntarily come streaming to the mountain of God's house in Jerusalem (Mic. 4:1–2), war will cease (Isa. 2:4), and all humanity will live without fear (Mic. 4:4).

Keep in mind that it is not required that all humanity *become* Israel. In today's terms, that means that not all are required to become Jewish. They will simply realize the truth of monotheism. And here is a critical distinction. All humanity will recognize the unity of God as a *result* of the final redemption, not as a *prerequisite* for it. This reflects the nonexistence of mission in the Hebrew Bible. Humanity will eventually come around to realizing the unity of God of its own accord. That realization of monotheism is paired organically with ethics, according to the Bible. The rules for providing for the poor and the stranger, demanding respect for parents, requiring just weights and measures and fair judgment in courts of law, forbidding fraud and robbery and taking vengeance, are all followed by the phrase, "I am the Lord" (Leviticus 19). The One Great God is simultaneously God of judgment and God of mercy, but never God of whim or caprice or fancy. The God of the Hebrew Bible insists on ethical behavior and compassion to the needy. True monotheists, therefore, must always aspire to these noble behaviors. There is a direct link between human behavior and reward or punishment.

Redemption is closely associated with the messianic hope. But in the Hebrew Bible, the messiah is a *symbol* of redemption rather than the *bringer* of redemption. The Hebrew word for "messiah," *mashiach,* means "anointed one." Anointing or rubbing the head or skin with oil was a way to heal damaged skin, treat wounds, or simply moisten chapped skin (Isa. 1:6; Amos 6:6). The Hebrew word for ointment, *mishchah,* comes from the same root. Oil was a valuable commodity during biblical times, and expensive to produce. Its pleasant nature and high value probably made it a logical sign of office, so anointing became a symbol for inducting priests (Exod. 28:41), kings (1 Sam. 10:1), and prophets (1 Kings 19:16).[2] All of these are servants of God in the Hebrew Bible. They all have a role in ensuring that the people act out the divine will. Only God, however, will bring the final redemption. That final act will include the coming of a righteous Israelite king from the line of David (Jer. 23:5–6), but that messianic king will not bring the redemption himself. Even in the most mystical references to the symbols associated with the birth of a future Davidic ruler, the messianic king and God are separate entities: "The Zeal of the Lord of Hosts shall bring this to pass" (Isa. 9:1–6).

The New Testament: Jesus as Redemptive Messiah

Redemption is understood rather differently in the New Testament, which understands that the messiah is both human and God the Redeemer. The word *Christ* is a Greek translation of the Hebrew *mashiach* (anointed one). *Christos* is the actual term for *mashiach* used by the Jewish translators of the Hebrew Bible into the Greek version called the Septuagint that was translated some two centuries before the birth of Jesus, roughly during the second century BCE. In the Septuagint translation, each of the thirty-nine appearances of the Hebrew *mashiach* is rendered as *christos.* The Greek and the Hebrew have exactly the same meaning there: anyone who is anointed with oil. Later, as Christianity emerged in the first century CE, Jesus was recognized as the anointed one who was also the incarnation of God. In Christian usage, and when referring to Jesus, Messiah is capitalized as a reference to God in human form. In the Gospel of John, when Andrew meets Jesus, "the first thing he did was to find his brother Simon and say to him 'We have found the Messiah'" (John 2:41). According to the Gospel of John, that Messiah is God, as articulated through the mystical introduction in which the Word of God, which *is* God, became flesh (John 1:1–14). Later in the same Gospel, Jesus is represented as one with the Father (John 10:37–38, 14:7–11, 17:5, 11), which most Christians understand to mean that Jesus is God.

In the New Testament, therefore, Jesus, as both Messiah and God, is the bringer of redemption. Jesus himself is the divine Redeemer. He is understood to embody the fulfillment of the Hebrew Bible prophecies and paradigms, such as the suffering of Israel (Isa. 52:12–53:13), atonement for sin through sacrifice (Lev. 4, 5, 17:11), and the coming of God the Redeemer (Isa. 49:7, 59:20). The prophecies of the Hebrew Bible thus become harbingers of Jesus to Christians, and also become realized through the birth, mission, and passion of Christ. But Jesus died before a final divinely wrought redemption took place, so it is understood that the final redemption will occur at a future time in relation to Jesus's return as the redemptive Messiah, Christ the Redeemer. This is known in Greek as the Parousia, the "Second Coming of Christ."

There is a wide range of belief among Christians about what will occur in the process of that final divine redemption, but most agree that there will be a period of tribulation through which believers will experience worldwide persecution and be purified and strengthened by it, based on Matthew 24:15–22, Mark 13:14–20, and Luke 21:20–33. Most Christians also believe that Jesus Christ the Redeemer will return in the Second Coming after that tribulation, based on 2 Thessalonians 2:1–4. There will be a rapture, in which believers will be united with Jesus in heaven

(1 Thess. 4:16–17). There will also be a millennium, meaning a thousand-year period that will herald the imminent end of the world: "Then I saw an angel coming down from heaven, holding in his hand the key of the bottomless pit and a great chain. And he seized the dragon, that ancient serpent, who is the Devil and Satan, and bound him for a thousand years, and threw him into the pit, and shut it and sealed it over him, that he should deceive the nations no more, till the thousand years were ended. After that he must be loosed for a little while.... And when the thousand years are ended, Satan will be loosed from his prison and will come out to deceive the nations which are at the four corners of the earth" (Rev. 20:1–3, 7–8).

There are a number of differences among Christian beliefs over the order of events and the nature of the millennium described in the book of Revelation. This is an issue especially for conservative Protestants, whose different positions are sometimes identified as postmillennialism, amillennialism, and premillennialism. We are not concerned with the details here, but with the results. Who will benefit from the final redemption that will be brought about by the Second Coming?

As in the Hebrew Bible, the New Testament stresses the redemption of the community of believers. In some passages, only those who believe and are baptized will be saved, "but he who does not believe shall be condemned" (Mark 16:16). Other passages would extend the benefits to those outside the immediate community of believers, "for all alike have sinned and are deprived of the divine glory; and all are justified by God's free grace alone, through His act of liberation in the person of Christ Jesus" (Rom. 3:23–24). "The universe itself is to be freed from the shackles of mortality and is to enter upon the glorious liberty of the children of God" (Rom. 8:21).

Jesus's crucifixion in the New Testament is a redemptive sacrifice reminiscent of the redemptive sacrifices called the "guilt offerings" and "sin offerings" of Leviticus chapters 4 and 5. But as we have noted in the case of "merit of the ancestors," the redemption through Jesus's merit and sacrifice is far greater than the redemption from the sacrificial offerings found in the Hebrew Bible. Jesus gave his life "as a ransom for many" (Mark 10:45, Matt. 20:28). Some commentators have noted that "many" does not necessarily imply any kind of restriction, but the universal nature of this redemption is stressed in some passages of the New Testament, such as 1 Timothy 2:5–6: "For there is one God, and there is one mediator between God and man, Christ Jesus, himself man, who sacrificed himself to win freedom for all mankind, revealing God's purpose at God's good time." This sentiment is clear also in Acts 10:34–35: "Peter began: 'I now understand how true it is that God has no favorites, but that in every nation those who are God-fearing and do what is right are acceptable to Him.'"

Apocalyptic Revelation in the Qur'an

The Qur'an also contains references to sacrifice. We have already considered the Intended Sacrifice of Abraham's son. Sacrifice in the Qur'an, however, is a minor motif in general, and aside from the story of the near-sacrifice of Abraham's son, there is little emphasis on any redemptive nature of sacrifice. There are, however, a great number of references to the End of Days.

The Qur'an has a number of terms that relate to specific aspects of the End of Days, including the Last Day *(al-yawm al-akhir),* Day of Judgment *(yawm al-din),* and Day of Resurrection *(yawm al-qiyama).* As within the ancient Near Eastern culture of the Hebrew Bible, the indigenous people of Arabia to whom Muhammad preached seem not to have been familiar with a concept of an afterlife. The revelation that Muhammad received had to emphasize the notion and repeat it in a variety of ways in order to teach them the meaning of divine judgment and reward and punishment in the next world. Some have likened the entire Qur'an to an apocalyptic revelation because apocalyptic images are so prominent in it. The Qur'an is not organized chronologically or topically, however, so these many references occur throughout the scripture. Because they reflect a series of revelations that were given to Muhammad over some twenty-two years, they may appear at first to be somewhat inconsistent. Nevertheless, certain trends begin to emerge that may be summarized here.

The End of Days will arrive amid great disruptions in the natural order of things. The earth will convulse and shake (Qur'an 99), and the heavens will be split in two (82) and be rolled up: "When the sun is darkened, and when the stars fall, and the mountains are set moving, and when the camels are neglected, when the wild beasts are herded, and when the oceans are flooded, when souls are reunited, and when the infant girl that was buried [alive] is asked for what sin she was killed, when the pages are laid open and when the sky is stripped, when the Fire is ignited and when the Garden in drawn near, every soul will know what it has brought about" (81:1–14). Gog and Magog will be released (18:94), God will bring forth a beast from the center of the earth who will speak (27:82), and a trumpet or horn will sound and the dead will be called out from their graves for judgment (27:87, 36:51).

There is a clear demarcation between heaven (often referred to as *al-janna*, the "Garden") and hell (*jahannum* or *al-nar*, the "Fire"). Those who enter paradise are people who recognize God's signs, while those who reject them will experience eternal hellfire. Recognizing the signs of God is an idiom in the Qur'an for acknowledging the truth of monotheism, and this recognition includes more than simple faith. It includes engaging in righteous behavior, acting with integrity, doing good works, and praying to God. Rejecting God's signs is to deny God, lack humility, engage in evil behaviors, and scoff at the notion of a final judgment. Behavior is thus built into the notion of the recognition of the signs of God (7:35–58).

There is a strong view of resurrection in the Qur'an, and a detailed description of it can be found in chapter 39, verses 67–75 (and elsewhere). It includes a blowing of the trumpet (74:8) and the return of all dead to life, the gathering for judgment (6:38, 42:29) when everyone's personal book of behaviors will be laid open (17:13–14, 52:2–3), their deeds will be weighed on the scales of justice (7:8–9, 21:47), and all God's creatures will bear witness against themselves (6:130). The result will then be entrance into heaven or hell. In some passages, the judgment brings eternal damnation or salvation (4:169, 10:52, 13:35, 25:15). In others the time in hell is unspecified, so later Islamic writings disagreed over whether the punishment of damnation is eternal.

We noted how the notion of salvation in the English language is strongly influenced by Christian theology, and that an exact equivalent for the word does not exist in the Hebrew Bible. Neither is it found in the Qur'an, but other words convey similar ideas. One is the term *al-fawz al-`azim* (supreme success): "Whoever obeys God and His messenger will be entered into the Garden under which rivers flow, abiding there forever. That is the supreme success" (4:13). "God promises the believers, men and women, Gardens under which rivers flow, abiding there forever, pleasant dwelling is the Gardens of Eden—God's favor is best. This is the supreme success" (9:72). Believers are therefore "the successful" (9:20).

Another term with a meaning similar to *al-fawz al-`azim* is *muflihun* (the successful). On the day that God will call to them, those who have repented, believed, and done righteousness will be successful (28:67). They are a community that calls to the good, demanding good deeds and forbidding evil (2:104), who follow the light that has been sent down (7:157), and who seek God's countenance (30:38). God is pleased with them; they are the party of God (*hizbullah*) and will be brought into Gardens under which rivers flow, abiding there forever (59:22).

These descriptions apply most directly to the followers of divine revelation as articulated by his prophet Muhammad, but these are not the only ones who will be favored by God. According to the Qur'an, God saved all of his prophets. All of these prophets besides Muhammad lived long before the Qur'an was revealed, and they include Abraham, Jonah, Moses, and Lot, along with others that are not known from the Bible. One such prophet is Hud, about whom the Qur'an mentions, "We saved him and those with him by a mercy from Us, but We cut off the root of those who denied Our signs and were not believers" (7:72). Other prophets that God saved along with the righteous among their people are Salih (11:66) and Shu'ayb (11:94). Even the wife of the evil Pharaoh was saved by her belief: "God made an example with the wife of Pharaoh for those who believe, when she said, 'My Lord, build me a house in Your presence in the Garden and save me from Pharaoh and his acts. Deliver me from the evil nation" (66:11). This example and other verses extend redemption and salvation to righteous believers who are not official Muslims but who practice the same kind of ethical monotheism in their daily lives that is taught by Islam.

The heavy Qur'anic emphasis on redemption, judgment, and reward and punishment in an afterlife, and the varied language and images in these passages, have been read in a variety of ways by Muslim scholars. Some have come away from them with the belief that only those who follow God as articulated by the specific teachings of the Qur'an and the prophet Muhammad are entitled entry into heaven. Other learned scholars have understood the Qur'an to teach that anyone who does good works and believes in God and divine judgment merits entrance into paradise. Sometimes the same scriptural verses are cited to support both positions.

This phenomenon of inclusive redemption that extends beyond the immediate community of believers is common to all three families of monotheism. In each case, scripture associates redemption first with the community of believers who have dedicated their lives and often suffered in their loyalty to their religion. Recall that scripture reflects the earliest historical period of emerging religions when the believers suffered the most for their faithfulness and devotion to God and the emerging religious system. It is logical and reasonable for the authoritative core of the religious system to promise rewards for such dedicated allegiance and faithful devotion. In each scripture, however, there is also room for redemption or salvation for those who do not belong to the specific religious community. There is room in each to extend redemption beyond membership in the chosen community of God.

The religious literatures that emerged to interpret scripture in the generations following the revelations sometimes expanded the pool of those available to redemption. Sometimes they narrowed it. These are the interpretive literatures of Judaism, Christianity, and Islam, and they were always deeply influenced by the historical periods in which they were written. As usual, when the religious thinkers whose views are represented in them lived in a world of scarcity and competition and when life was difficult, they tended to narrow their view of those worthy of redemption. But when they lived in a world of plenty when life was good, they tended to be more generous in their assessment of those worthy of salvation. Perhaps it was God's design that every case of scriptural revelation allows for generosity or parsimoniousness.

Conclusion

Retaining Our Uniqueness while Affirming the Other

We have taken a long journey through the history of the notion of chosenness. We have observed its birth in the cauldron of ancient Near Eastern polytheisms and how it became a core part of the self-concept of one small community of monotheists. We have observed how it became an authoritative marker of authenticity in the polemics and arguments among competing expressions of monotheism, how chosenness became a category over which great arguments, inquisitions, and religious wars have been fought. We have observed how the notion of election triumphed along with the victory of monotheism as Christianity and Islam were established as imperial religions in the world's greatest empires. The notion of chosenness became a sine qua non of monotheism. We have observed how chosenness has been so deeply linked to monotheism that it is difficult to conceive of monotheism without the notion of true believers being in a special, intimate, and exclusive relationship with the One Great God.

But as I have tried to demonstrate in this book, chosenness and monotheism are not the same thing, nor are they dependent on one other. Their intimate relationship is actually an accident of the history of the religions that emerged out of the ancient Near East. As F. E. Peters has put it, "Monotheism avers that God is unique. Chosenness makes the believers unique." They are not the same thing, nor do they require one another. Some monotheists within each of the three great monotheist traditions transcend the elitism

of chosenness and still believe in the absolute unity and universal-
ity of the One Great God. Unfortunately, they tend to be atypical
and are relatively rare.

Were all of humanity to believe in the same kind of monotheism, or even if all *monotheists* were to believe in the same kind of
monotheism, then we would all belong to the same community in
chosen communion with God. If this were to occur and all were to
consider themselves part of the same elect community, then perhaps
the elitism of chosenness would disappear and the tensions that
lead people to bicker, brawl, and sometimes go to war would end.

But humanity has never believed in the same kind of monotheism. The human species seems to have been created in such a way
that its members simply and naturally argue. They inevitably have
different opinions and disagree with each other. The human condition seems to be that we see things differently from one another, and
we feel entitled to our own opinions and our own perceptions. Even
those who grew up in the same household with the same family education and the same religious experiences, education, and training
often have very different views of God, humanity, and the universe.

Was humanity created to be contrary? I personally doubt
whether that would have been part of the great design. But as noted
at the very beginning of this book, Genesis 1:26 remains one of the
most interesting and perplexing verses of any scripture: "God said,
'Let us make human beings in our image, after our likeness'" I seri-
ously doubt whether humans were created for the purpose of being
stubborn, but I am convinced that we were created with the potential for independent thinking. Part of our "divine image" is that we
are sentient, alert, and attentive beings. Unlike simple machines or
even complex computers, every human was created with a unique
essence and extraordinary individuality that is deeply embedded in
our processing mechanisms. We reflect as we process the world
around us. We tend to think independently as we wonder at the
beauty of creation, and we ponder the meaning of existence. Given
that these traits reflect our deepest and most basic nature, how
could it possibly be that we were created otherwise? Should it be

surprising to the Creator that our human need to think independently would prevent us from agreeing even about the nature of our own creation?

The origin of human individuality and contrariness is a conundrum that we are unlikely to resolve, a mystery for which human experience will never find a definitive answer. We are unable to agree on the answer because we continue to think about the nature of our existence in new ways. Even the greatest theologians have not been able to agree on the nature of our human relationship with eternity, or even on the nature of human existence. An old Jewish tradition compares the creation of coinage with the creation of God's creatures. The likeness of the king, or the emperor or caliph, on the coin appears the same for every one of the thousands or millions of coins that are stamped into existence. But the likeness and nature of every single individual creature of God is unique. There are no two alike.

With adequate awareness of this awesome difference we can only realize our humility in the presence of the Creator of the universe. Each of our religious traditions reflects the truth of God and of God's creation. Each scripture is a revelation of the divine message. But even if every single word were the exact enunciation of God, we would disagree over each meaning. I can only consider this awesome individuality to be part of the divine plan.

As a Jew, I grew up within one of many religious systems that have emerged through this mystery of human creation. I count myself to be a believing member of my religious tradition, and I consider it a pathway to truth. But I have enough experience in studying other religious paths to transcend the naïveté that only I have the keys to truth—that only I and those who agree with me know the code that will allow us to pass through the door to redemption. I know too many people much wiser than me who follow a different path and from whom I have learned great wisdom.

I do consider myself a member of a religious community that is in a relationship of chosenness with God. But that does not mean that God is choosy as I might be about ice cream or chocolate. Chosenness need not be limiting.

My religious community is unique. There is no other like it. And *within* my community I count myself a member of one subgroup of believers, among many others, that is unique despite so many similarities within my larger religious affiliation. We are uniquely different than many others within the community. And I count myself a unique individual within my subgroup. There is no other individual who seems to have exactly the same perspective as I have. No one sees the world quite like me, or quite like you.

An old dictum teaches that a minority of one is only a fool. But we are all, when naked and alone at the end of our natural lives, a minority of one. No matter what we profess, our essential, unique, individual nature is known only to the One who created all.

In the same way that we are unique in our individuality, we are also unique in our small communities, and in those conglomerates of communities that make up our unique religious affiliations. Every religion is unique, and each has access to wisdom, including wisdom about God and eternity. But no religion has wisdom about which all of us can agree, and none has the right to be confident that it has a monopoly on truth. If God created everyone to be absolutely unique, are we not all chosen?

Notes

Introduction

1. His complete definition is

"CHOOSE, v.t. 1. To pick out; to select; to take by way of preference from two or more things offered; to make choice of. The man the Lord doth choose shall be holy. Num. 16. 2. To take in preference. Let us choose to us judgment. Job 34. 3. To prefer; to choose for imitation; to follow. Envy not the oppressor, and choose none of his ways. Prov. 3. 4. To elect for eternal happiness; to predestinate to life. Many are called but few chosen. Matt. 20. For his elects sake, whom he hath chosen. Mark 13. 5. To elect or designate to office or employment by votes or suffrages. In the United States, the people choose representatives by votes, usually by ballot."

2. For the Hebrew Bible, my references were *Tanakh: The Holy Scriptures. The New JPS Translation According to the Traditional Hebrew Text*, edited by Harry Orlinsky, E. A. Speiser, and H. R. Ginsberg (Philadelphia: Jewish Publication Society, 1982), and *The Oxford Study Bible*, edited by M. Jack Suggs, Katharine Doob Sakenfeld, and James R. Mueller (New York: Oxford University Press, 1992). For the Qur'an, I consulted the translations of Marmaduke Pickthall, *The Glorious Qur'an*, bilingual edition with English translation (Istanbul: Enes Matbaasi, 1999); Muhammad Asad, *The Message of the Qur'an* (Gibraltar: Dar al-Andalus,

1980); and Thomas Cleary, *The Qur'an: A New Translation* (Chicago: Starlatch Press, 2004).

3. *The Oxford Study Bible* (New York: Oxford University Press, 1992); The Cambridge Study Bible (Cambridge: Cambridge University Press, 1993).

Chapter 1

1. The Hebrew Bible is the collection of biblical texts that Christians refer to as the Old Testament. I prefer the former term because it is neutral. "Old Testament" refers to the old testimony of God's covenant with the Jews, which was superseded by the "New Testament" of God's covenant with those who have chosen Christ: "By speaking of a new covenant, He has pronounced the first one old; and anything that is growing old and aging will shortly disappear" (Heb. 8:6–13).

2. In Jewish religious tradition, the word *Israel* refers to the Jewish people. The official name of the modern nation-state is Medinat Yisrael, meaning the "State of Israel" or "Nation-state of the Jews."

Chapter 2

1. As a result, any absolutely correct pronunciation is unlikely today. It became custom, then, to substitute the word *Lord*, both in the Hebrew and in most biblical translations, for the name that is sometimes called the tetragrammaton, meaning the four-letter name of God.

2. BCE (before the common era) and CE (the common era) are the standard means for marking the current Western calendar. They are preferred to BC (before Christ) and AD (anno Domini) because the latter conveys a theology that is not accepted by all people who use the dating system.

3. James B. Pritchard, *The Ancient Near East: An Anthology of Texts and Pictures* (Princeton: Princeton University Press, 1975), 2:168.

4. There is one striking exception in the biblical book of Ruth, which is extraordinary for Ruth's loyalty to her mother-in-law and willingness to abandon her own people and gods when she proclaimed, "… your people shall be my people, and your God my God" (Ruth 1:16).

5. For more examples of this firm commitment, see Deuteronomy 4:35, 39; 1 Kings 8:60; Isaiah 23:10, 45:6, 18, 21.

6. For more on Akhenaten, see Erik Horning, *Akhenaten and the Religion of Light,* translated by David Lorton (Ithaca, NY: Cornell University Press, 1999), 87–94, or Donald Redford, "The Monotheism of

Akhenaten," in Hershel Shanks and Jack Meinhardt, *Aspects of Monotheism* (Washington, DC: Biblical Archaeology Society, 1996), 11–26. For some studies about other experiments in monotheism in the ancient world, see Polymnia Athanassiadi and Michael Frede, *Pagan Monotheism in Late Antiquity* (Oxford: Oxford University Press, 1991), and G. R. Hawting, *The Idea of Idolatry and the Emergence of Islam: From Polemic to History* (Cambridge: Cambridge University Press), 1999.

7. This valley, called *gey ben-hinnom* or *gey hinnom* in Hebrew, became associated with the burning of children, which in later times became associated with hell or *gehenna* (*jahannum* in Arabic). For the relevant biblical sources, see Leviticus 18:21, 20:2–4; Deuteronomy 18:10; 2 Kings 16:3, 17:17, 21:6, 23:10; Jeremiah 7:31, 19:5; Ezekiel 16:21, 20:31, 23:37, 39; Psalms 106:37–38.

8. Niels Peter Lemche, *The Canaanites and Their Land: The Tradition of the Canaanites* (Sheffield, UK: JSOT Press, 1991), 25–62.

9. My translation here is influenced by Everett Fox, *The Five Books of Moses: A New Translation* (New York: Schocken, 1995), 885.

10. Pritchard, *The Ancient Near East*, 1:194. Because these are translations from ancient texts that often have parts missing and use words and terms that do not translate word-for-word into English, editorial marks are used in the translation to indicate these aspects of the original. Square brackets indicate restorations in the text, and parentheses mark interpolations made for a better understanding in translation.

11. Prichard, *The Ancient Near East*, 1:206–208.

Chapter 3

1. See Rodney Stark and Laurence R. Iannaccone, "A Supply-Side Reinterpretation of the 'Secularization' of Europe," *Journal for the Scientific Study of Religion* 33 (1994): 230–252; Rodney Stark, "How New Religions Succeed: A Theoretical Model," in *The Future of New Religious Movements*, ed. by David G. Bromley and Phillip E. Hammond (Macon, GA: Mercer University Press, 1987), 11–19; Rodney Stark and William Sims Bainbridge, *A Theory of Religion* (Rutgers, NJ: Rutgers University Press, 1996).

2. H. L. Ginsberg, *Kitbe Ugarit* (Jerusalem: Bialik, 1936); T. H. Gaster, "Psalm 29," *Jewish Quarterly Review* 37 (1946–47): 55ff; F. M. Cross, "Notes on a Canaanite Psalm in the Old Testament," *BASOR* 117 (1950): 19–21; Carola Kloos, *Yhwh's Combat with the Sea* (Leiden: Brill, 1986).

3. John Gager, *The Origins of Anti-Semitism* (New York: Oxford, 1985), 39, 69.

4. Rabbinic literature includes more than the Talmud, but the Talmud is the core text. The Jewish Kara'ites never accepted the authority of the Talmud. They number only some thirty thousand people today, most of whom live in Israel.

5. There are some difficulties associated with the scriptural status of the Talmud. The Talmudic sage is different from the prophet, for example, and the nature of the Talmud is clearly interpretive in direct relation to the Hebrew Bible. It might be phenomenologically termed "quasi-scripture," but its title as Oral Torah among Jews *(torah shebe'al peh)* gives it authority for keeping the finite and canonized revelation of the Hebrew Bible alive in a manner that finds clear parallels with the title and role of the New Testament.

Chapter 4

1. Richard Horsley, "Popular Messianic Movements around the Time of Jesus," *Catholic Biblical Quarterly* 46 (1984): 471–495.

2. Paul W. Harkins, trans., *The Fathers of the Church: St. John Chrysostom Discourses against Judaizing Christians* (Washington, DC: Catholic University of America Press, 1977).

Chapter 6

1. The Hebrew letter *hey* is the article that makes a noun definite. All the other days mentioned during the creation process in Genesis 1 are referred to as "a first day," "a second day," and the like. Only the sixth day is written as "*the* sixth day," rather than "*a* sixth day." There is significance to that difference, according to a third-century rabbinic sage named Resh Lakish, and the message is that God is announcing to the world the future creation of Israel, who will hold fast to God's word.

2. Avot de Rabbi Natan in the two versions (in Hebrew) (Vienna: Schechter, 1887), ver. 2, chap. 44, p. 124.

3. The firstborn son is typically preferred for blessing and inheritance in the Hebrew Bible.

Chapter 7

1. The purification ritual of the red heifer occurs in Numbers 19, which is immediately followed by the statement that Miriam died in the Desert of Zin, in Numbers 20:1.

2. Mekhilta de Rabbi Yishma'el *devayehi* 3 (Jerusalem: Horowitz-Rabin, 1970), 99.

3. Leviticus Rabba 36, 6.

4. The significance of the Zechariah verse lies in the act of blowing the ram's horn (*shofar*, in Hebrew), which is a central part of the atonement service and ritual in the Jewish confessional prayers on the holiest day in the Jewish calendar, Yom Kippur (the Day of Atonement). The sages connect the ram's horn of Yom Kippur with the redemptive ram in the story of the Binding in Genesis 22.

5. There exists a countertradition in the New Testament that states that good works are required, in addition to faith (James 2:1–26). A certain tension may be found there between grace and good works, as demonstrated by the inclusion of such passages as Matthew 5:17 alongside the story of the prodigal son in Luke 15:11–32. The thrust of the New Testament view, however, is firmly in the camp of divine grace.

6. This story is told a half-dozen times in slightly different versions. The following is a composite from two versions found in *Sahih Al-Bukhari, Book of Commentaries* (Book 60), numbers 3 and 236. They can be found in a bilingual edition of Muhammad Muhsin Khan, *The Translation of the Meanings of Sahih Al-Bukhari* (Lahore: Kazi, 1983), 6:3–5, 198–201.

7. A number of traditions point out that Abraham told three lies in his lifetime.

8. Ismail Ibn Kathir, *Tafsir al-Qur'an al-'Azim* (Cairo: 'Isa al-Babi al-Halabi, n.d.), 4:18.

Chapter 8

1. An exception might be the prophet Elijah in 2 Kings, chapter 2, but he is not depicted as entering heaven after his death. Rather, he was miraculously taken up alive in a whirlwind as a symbol of his extraordinary prophetic status.

2. Other references from the Hebrew Bible, such as the image of the dry bones in Ezekiel 37, are taken by Bible scholars to be only metaphors. In the case of the Ezekiel passage, the image is a metaphor for the political revival of the Israelite state.

3. David Biale, *Power and Powerlessness in Jewish History* (New York: Schocken, 1986), 11–12.

4. The modern state of Israel has indeed harnessed the apparatus of state to promote its Jewish national and political agenda, but not the religion of Judaism. Muslims and Christians in the modern state of Israel are legally free to practice their religion without government interference.

Chapter 9

1. In both of these verses, the Hebrew says, literally, that God has "redeemed my soul from all adversity." The use of the word *soul* is a Hebrew idiomatic expression that does not equal the notion of a soul within the body that is common today. That notion of division between body and soul does not exist in the Hebrew Bible but is a legacy of Hellenistic thinking. The Hebrew term, *nefesh*, which is often translated as "soul," actually means "self," and an absolutely literal (but somewhat awkward) translation would be God "redeemed my self from all adversity."

2. All kings were anointed *(mashiach)*, including kings who were considered to be evil in the eyes of God, and even the Persian king Cyrus was called by God "my anointed" (Isa. 45:1).

Suggestions for Further Reading

Brown, Brian Arthur. *Noah's Other Son: Bridging the Gap Between the Bible and the Qur'an*. New York: Continuum, 2007.

Cook, Michael J. *Modern Jews Engage the New Testament: Enhancing Jewish Well-Being in a Christian Environment*. Woodstock, VT: Jewish Lights Publishing, 2008.

Coppola, David L., ed. *What Do We Want the Other to Teach about Us? Jewish, Christian, and Muslim Dialogues*. Fairfield, CT: Sacred Heart University Press, 2006.

Gillman, Neil. *The Jewish Approach to God: A Brief Introduction for Christians*. Woodstock, VT: Jewish Lights Publishing, 2003.

Heckman, Bud, ed. *InterActive Faith: The Essential Interreligious Community-Building Handbook*. Woodstock, VT: SkyLight Paths, 2008.

Henderson, John B. *The Construction of Orthodoxy and Heresy: Neo-Confucian, Islamic, Jewish, and Early Christian Patterns*. Albany, NY: State University of New York Press, 1998.

Idliby, Ranya, Suzanne Oliver, and Priscilla Warner. *The Faith Club: A Muslim, A Christian, A Jew—Three Women Search for Understanding*. New York: Free Press, 2006.

Korn, Eugene B., and John T. Pawlikowski. *Two Faiths, One Covenant? Jewish and Christian Identity in the Presence of the Other*. New York: Rowman and Littlefield, 2005.

Lederach, John Paul. *The Moral Imagination: The Art and Soul of Building Peace*. New York: Oxford University Press, 2005.

Miller, Edward W. *Vision of Abraham: The Intertwined Stories of Islam and Judaism Told through Images*. Beltsville, MD: Amana Publications, n.d.

Nasr, Seyyed Hossein. *Knowledge and the Sacred*. Albany, NY: State University of New York Press, 1989.

Peters, F. E. *The Monotheists: Jews, Christians, and Muslims in Conflict and Competition*. 2 Vols. Princeton, NJ: Princeton University Press, 2003.

Sacks, Jonathan. *The Dignity of Difference: How to Avoid the Clash of Civilizations*. London: Continuum, 2002.

Smoch, David R., ed. *Interfaith Dialogue and Peacebuilding*. Washington, DC: US Institute of Peace Press, 2002.

Stark, Rodney, and Roger Finke. *Acts of Faith: Explaining the Human Side of Religion*. Los Angeles: University of California Press, 2000.

Swidler, Leonard, Khaled Duran and Reuven Firestone. *Jews, Christians, Muslims in Dialogue: A Practical Handbook*. New London, CT: Twenty-Third Publications, 2007.

Swidler, Leonard, and Paul Mojzes. *The Study of Religion in an Age of Global Dialogue*. Philadelphia: Temple University Press, 2000.

Zagorin, Perez. *How the Idea of Religious Toleration Came to the West*. Princeton: Princeton University Press, 2003.

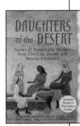

Spiritual Practice

Soul Fire: Accessing Your Creativity *by Rev. Thomas Ryan, CSP*
Shows you how to cultivate your creative spirit as a way to encourage personal growth.
6 x 9, 160 pp, Quality PB, 978-1-59473-243-0 **$16.99**

Running—The Sacred Art: Preparing to Practice
by Dr. Warren A. Kay; Foreword by Kristin Armstrong
Examines how your daily run can enrich your spiritual life.
5½ x 8½, 160 pp, Quality PB, 978-1-59473-227-0 **$16.99**

Hospitality—The Sacred Art: Discovering the Hidden Spiritual Power
of Invitation and Welcome *by Rev. Nanette Sawyer; Foreword by Rev. Dirk Ficca*
Explores how this ancient spiritual practice can transform your relationships.
5½ x 8½, 192 pp, Quality PB, 978-1-59473-228-7 **$16.99**

Thanking & Blessing—The Sacred Art: Spiritual Vitality through
Gratefulness *by Jay Marshall, PhD; Foreword by Philip Gulley*
Offers practical tips for uncovering the blessed wonder in our lives—even in trying circumstances. 5½ x 8½, 176 pp, Quality PB, 978-1-59473-231-7 **$16.99**

Everyday Herbs in Spiritual Life: A Guide to Many Practices
by Michael J. Caduto; Foreword by Rosemary Gladstar Explores the power of herbs.
7 x 9, 208 pp, 21 b/w illustrations, Quality PB, 978-1-59473-174-7 **$16.99**

Divining the Body: Reclaim the Holiness of Your Physical Self *by Jan Phillips*
8 x 8, 256 pp, Quality PB, 978-1-59473-080-1 **$16.99**

Finding Time for the Timeless: Spirituality in the Workweek
by John McQuiston II Simple stories show you how refocus your daily life.
5½ x 6¾, 208 pp, HC, 978-1-59473-035-1 **$17.99**

The Gospel of Thomas: A Guidebook for Spiritual Practice
by Ron Miller; Translations by Stevan Davies
6 x 9, 160 pp, Quality PB, 978-1-59473-047-4 **$14.99**

Earth, Water, Fire, and Air: Essential Ways of Connecting to Spirit
by Cait Johnson 6 x 9, 224 pp, HC, 978-1-893361-65-2 **$19.95**

Labyrinths from the Outside In: Walking to Spiritual Insight—A Beginner's Guide
by Donna Schaper and Carole Ann Camp
6 x 9, 208 pp, b/w illus. and photos, Quality PB, 978-1-893361-18-8 **$16.95**

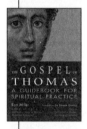

Practicing the Sacred Art of Listening: A Guide to Enrich Your Relationships
and Kindle Your Spiritual Life—The Listening Center Workshop
by Kay Lindahl 8 x 8, 176 pp, Quality PB, 978-1-893361-85-0 **$16.95**

Releasing the Creative Spirit: Unleash the Creativity in Your Life
by Dan Wakefield 7 x 10, 256 pp, Quality PB, 978-1-893361-36-2 **$16.95**

The Sacred Art of Bowing: Preparing to Practice
by Andi Young 5½ x 8½, 128 pp, b/w illus., Quality PB, 978-1-893361-82-9 **$14.95**

The Sacred Art of Chant: Preparing to Practice
by Ana Hernández 5½ x 8½, 192 pp, Quality PB, 978-1-59473-036-8 **$15.99**

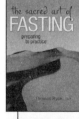

The Sacred Art of Fasting: Preparing to Practice
by Thomas Ryan, CSP 5½ x 8½, 192 pp, Quality PB, 978-1-59473-078-8 **$15.99**

The Sacred Art of Forgiveness: Forgiving Ourselves and Others through God's Grace
by Marcia Ford 8 x 8, 176 pp, Quality PB, 978-1-59473-175-4 **$16.99**

The Sacred Art of Listening: Forty Reflections for Cultivating a Spiritual Practice
by Kay Lindahl; Illustrations by Amy Schnapper
8 x 8, 160 pp, b/w illus., Quality PB, 978-1-893361-44-7 **$16.99**

The Sacred Art of Lovingkindness: Preparing to Practice
by Rabbi Rami Shapiro; Foreword by Marcia Ford 5½ x 8½, 176 pp, Quality PB, 978-1-59473-151-8 **$16.99**

Sacred Speech: A Practical Guide for Keeping Spirit in Your Speech
by Rev. Donna Schaper 6 x 9, 176 pp, Quality PB, 978-1-59473-068-9 **$15.99**
HC, 978-1-893361-74-4 **$21.95**

Sacred Texts—SkyLight Illuminations Series

Offers today's spiritual seeker an accessible entry into the great classic texts of the world's spiritual traditions. Each classic is presented in an accessible translation, with facing pages of guided commentary from experts, giving you the keys you need to understand the history, context and meaning of the text. This series enables you, whatever your background, to experience and understand classic spiritual texts directly, and to make them a part of your life.

CHRISTIANITY

The End of Days: Essential Selections from Apocalyptic Texts—
Annotated & Explained *Annotation by Robert G. Clouse*
Helps you understand the complex Christian visions of the end of the world.
5½ x 8½, 224 pp, Quality PB, 978-1-59473-170-9 **$16.99**

The Hidden Gospel of Matthew: Annotated & Explained
Translation & Annotation by Ron Miller
Takes you deep into the text cherished around the world to discover the words and events that have the strongest connection to the historical Jesus.
5½ x 8½, 272 pp, Quality PB, 978-1-59473-038-2 **$16.99**

The Lost Sayings of Jesus: Teachings from Ancient Christian, Jewish, Gnostic and Islamic Sources—Annotated & Explained
Translation & Annotation by Andrew Phillip Smith; Foreword by Stephan A. Hoeller
This collection of more than three hundred sayings depicts Jesus as a Wisdom teacher who speaks to people of all faiths as a mystic and spiritual master.
5½ x 8½, 240 pp, Quality PB, 978-1-59473-172-3 **$16.99**

Philokalia: The Eastern Christian Spiritual Texts—Selections Annotated & Explained *Annotation by Allyne Smith; Translation by G. E. H. Palmer, Phillip Sherrard and Bishop Kallistos Ware*
The first approachable introduction to the wisdom of the Philokalia, which is the classic text of Eastern Christian spirituality.
5½ x 8½, 240 pp, Quality PB, 978-1-59473-103-7 **$16.99**

The Sacred Writings of Paul: Selections Annotated & Explained
Translation & Annotation by Ron Miller
Explores the apostle Paul's core message of spiritual equality, freedom and joy.
5½ x 8½, 224 pp, Quality PB, 978-1-59473-213-3 **$16.99**

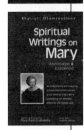

Sex Texts from the Bible: Selections Annotated & Explained
Translation & Annotation by Teresa J. Hornsby; Foreword by Amy-Jill Levine
Offers surprising insight into our modern sexual lives.
5½ x 8½, 208 pp, Quality PB, 978-1-59473-217-1 **$16.99**

Spiritual Writings on Mary: Annotated & Explained
Annotation by Mary Ford-Grabowsky; Foreword by Andrew Harvey
Examines the role of Mary, the mother of Jesus, as a source of inspiration in history and in life today. 5½ x 8½, 288 pp, Quality PB, 978-1-59473-001-6 **$16.99**

The Way of a Pilgrim: The Jesus Prayer Journey—Annotated & Explained
Translation & Annotation by Gleb Pokrovsky; Foreword by Andrew Harvey
This classic of Russian spirituality is the delightful account of one man who sets out to learn the prayer of the heart, also known as the "Jesus prayer."
5½ x 8½, 160 pp, Illus., Quality PB, 978-1-893361-31-7 **$14.95**

Sacred Texts—cont.

MORMONISM

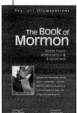

The Book of Mormon: Selections Annotated & Explained
Annotation by Jana Riess; Foreword by Phyllis Tickle
Explores the sacred epic that is cherished by more than twelve million members of the LDS church as the keystone of their faith.
5½ x 8½ , 272 pp, Quality PB, 978-1-59473-076-4 **$16.99**

NATIVE AMERICAN

Native American Stories of the Sacred: Annotated & Explained
Retold & Annotated by Evan T. Pritchard
Intended for more than entertainment, these teaching tales contain elegantly simple illustrations of time-honored truths.
5½ x 8½, 272 pp, Quality PB, 978-1-59473-112-9 **$16.99**

GNOSTICISM

Gnostic Writings on the Soul: Annotated & Explained
Translation & Annotation by Andrew Phillip Smith; Foreword by Stephan A. Hoeller
Reveals the inspiring ways your soul can remember and return to its unique, divine purpose.
5½ x 8½, 144 pp, Quality PB, 978-1-59473-220-1 **$16.99**

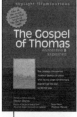

The Gospel of Philip: Annotated & Explained
Translation & Annotation by Andrew Phillip Smith; Foreword by Stevan Davies
Reveals otherwise unrecorded sayings of Jesus and fragments of Gnostic mythology.
5½ x 8½, 160 pp, Quality PB, 978-1-59473-111-2 **$16.99**

The Gospel of Thomas: Annotated & Explained
Translation & Annotation by Stevan Davies Sheds new light on the origins of Christianity and portrays Jesus as a wisdom-loving sage.
5½ x 8½, 192 pp, Quality PB, 978-1-893361-45-4 **$16.99**

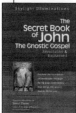

The Secret Book of John: The Gnostic Gospel—Annotated & Explained
Translation & Annotation by Stevan Davies The most significant and influential text of the ancient Gnostic religion.
5½ x 8½, 208 pp, Quality PB, 978-1-59473-082-5 **$16.99**

JUDAISM

The Divine Feminine in Biblical Wisdom Literature
Selections Annotated & Explained
Translation & Annotation by Rabbi Rami Shapiro; Foreword by Rev. Cynthia Bourgeault, PhD
Uses the Hebrew books of Psalms, Proverbs, Song of Songs, Ecclesiastes and Job, Wisdom literature and the Wisdom of Solomon to clarify who Wisdom is.
5½ x 8½, 240 pp, Quality PB, 978-1-59473-109-9 **$16.99**

Ethics of the Sages: Pirke Avot—Annotated & Explained
Translation & Annotation by Rabbi Rami Shapiro Clarifies the ethical teachings of the early Rabbis. 5½ x 8½, 192 pp, Quality PB, 978-1-59473-207-2 **$16.99**

Hasidic Tales: Annotated & Explained
Translation & Annotation by Rabbi Rami Shapiro
Introduces the legendary tales of the impassioned Hasidic rabbis, presenting them as stories rather than as parables. 5½ x 8½, 240 pp, Quality PB, 978-1-893361-86-7 **$16.95**

The Hebrew Prophets: Selections Annotated & Explained
Translation & Annotation by Rabbi Rami Shapiro; Foreword by Zalman M. Schachter-Shalomi
Focuses on the central themes covered by all the Hebrew prophets.
5½ x 8½, 224 pp, Quality PB, 978-1-59473-037-5 **$16.99**

Zohar: Annotated & Explained *Translation & Annotation by Daniel C. Matt*
The best-selling author of *The Essential Kabbalah* brings together in one place the most important teachings of the Zohar, the canonical text of Jewish mystical tradition.
5½ x 8½, 176 pp, Quality PB, 978-1-893361-51-5 **$15.99**

Sacred Texts—cont.

ISLAM

The Qur'an and Sayings of Prophet Muhammad
Selections Annotated & Explained
Annotation by Sohaib N. Sultan; Translation by Yusuf Ali; Revised by Sohaib N. Sultan
Foreword by Jane I. Smith
Explores how the timeless wisdom of the Qur'an can enrich your own spiritual journey.
5½ x 8½, 256 pp, Quality PB, 978-1-59473-222-5 **$16.99**

Rumi and Islam: Selections from His Stories, Poems, and Discourses—Annotated & Explained
Translation & Annotation by Ibrahim Gamard
Focuses on Rumi's place within the Sufi tradition of Islam, providing insight into the mystical side of the religion.
5½ x 8½, 240 pp, Quality PB, 978-1-59473-002-3 **$15.99**

EASTERN RELIGIONS

The Art of War—Spirituality for Conflict
Annotated & Explained
by Sun Tzu; Annotation by Thomas Huynh; Translation by Thomas Huynh and the Editors at Sonshi.com; Foreword by Marc Benioff; Preface by Thomas Cleary
Highlights principles that encourage a perceptive and spiritual approach to conflict.
5½ x 8½, 256 pp, Quality PB, 978-1-59473-244-7 **$16.99**

Bhagavad Gita: Annotated & Explained
Translation by Shri Purohit Swami; Annotation by Kendra Crossen Burroughs
Explains references and philosophical terms, shares the interpretations of famous spiritual leaders and scholars, and more.
5½ x 8½, 192 pp, Quality PB, 978-1-893361-28-7 **$16.95**

Dhammapada: Annotated & Explained
Translation by Max Müller and revised by Jack Maguire; Annotation by Jack Maguire
Contains all of Buddhism's key teachings.
5½ x 8½, 160 pp, b/w photos, Quality PB, 978-1-893361-42-3 **$14.95**

Selections from the Gospel of Sri Ramakrishna
Annotated & Explained
Translation by Swami Nikhilananda; Annotation by Kendra Crossen Burroughs
Introduces the fascinating world of the Indian mystic and the universal appeal of his message.
5½ x 8½, 240 pp, b/w photos, Quality PB, 978-1-893361-46-1 **$16.95**

Tao Te Ching: Annotated & Explained
Translation & Annotation by Derek Lin; Foreword by Lama Surya Das
Introduces an Eastern classic in an accessible, poetic and completely original way.
5½ x 8½, 192 pp, Quality PB, 978-1-59473-204-1 **$16.99**

STOICISM

The Meditations of Marcus Aurelius
Selections Annotated & Explained
Annotation by Russell McNeil, PhD; Translation by George Long; Revised by Russell McNeil, PhD
Offers insightful and engaging commentary into the historical background of Stoicism.
5½ x 8½, 288 pp, Quality PB, 978-1-59473-236-2 **$16.99**

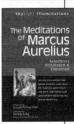

Spirituality of the Seasons

Autumn: A Spiritual Biography of the Season
Edited by Gary Schmidt and Susan M. Felch; Illustrations by Mary Azarian
Rejoice in autumn as a time of preparation and reflection. Includes Wendell Berry, David James Duncan, Robert Frost, A. Bartlett Giamatti, E. B. White, P. D. James, Julian of Norwich, Garret Keizer, Tracy Kidder, Anne Lamott, May Sarton.
6 x 9, 320 pp, 5 b/w illus., Quality PB, 978-1-59473-118-1 **$18.99**

Spring: A Spiritual Biography of the Season
Edited by Gary Schmidt and Susan M. Felch; Illustrations by Mary Azarian
Explore the gentle unfurling of spring and reflect on how nature celebrates rebirth and renewal. Includes Jane Kenyon, Lucy Larcom, Harry Thurston, Nathaniel Hawthorne, Noel Perrin, Annie Dillard, Martha Ballard, Barbara Kingsolver, Dorothy Wordsworth, Donald Hall, David Brill, Lionel Basney, Isak Dinesen, Paul Laurence Dunbar. 6 x 9, 352 pp, 6 b/w illus., Quality PB, 978-1-59473-246-1 **$18.99**

Summer: A Spiritual Biography of the Season
Edited by Gary Schmidt and Susan M. Felch; Illustrations by Barry Moser
"A sumptuous banquet.... These selections lift up an exquisite wholeness found within an everyday sophistication."— ★ *Publishers Weekly* starred review
Includes Anne Lamott, Luci Shaw, Ray Bradbury, Richard Selzer, Thomas Lynch, Walt Whitman, Carl Sandburg, Sherman Alexie, Madeleine L'Engle, Jamaica Kincaid.
6 x 9, 304 pp, 5 b/w illus., Quality PB, 978-1-59473-183-9 **$18.99**
HC, 978-1-59473-083-2 **$21.99**

Winter: A Spiritual Biography of the Season
Edited by Gary Schmidt and Susan M. Felch; Illustrations by Barry Moser
"This outstanding anthology features top-flight nature and spirituality writers on the fierce, inexorable season of winter.... Remarkably lively and warm, despite the icy subject." — ★ *Publishers Weekly* starred review
Includes Will Campbell, Rachel Carson, Annie Dillard, Donald Hall, Ron Hansen, Jane Kenyon, Jamaica Kincaid, Barry Lopez, Kathleen Norris, John Updike, E. B. White.
6 x 9, 288 pp, 6 b/w illus., Deluxe PB w/flaps, 978-1-893361-92-8 **$18.95**
HC, 978-1-893361-53-9 **$21.95**

Spirituality / Animal Companions

Blessing the Animals: Prayers and Ceremonies to Celebrate God's Creatures, Wild and Tame *Edited by Lynn L. Caruso* 5¼ x 7¼, 256 pp, HC, 978-1-59473-145-7 **$19.99**

Remembering My Pet: A Kid's Own Spiritual Workbook for When a Pet Dies
by Nechama Liss-Levinson, PhD, and Rev. Molly Phinney Baskette, MDiv; Foreword by Lynn L. Caruso
8 x 10, 48 pp, 2-color text, HC, 978-1-59473-221-3 **$16.99**

What Animals Can Teach Us about Spirituality: Inspiring Lessons from Wild and Tame Creatures *by Diana L. Guerrero* 6 x 9, 176 pp, Quality PB, 978-1-893361-84-3 **$16.95**

Spirituality—A Week Inside

Come and Sit: A Week Inside Meditation Centers
by Marcia Z. Nelson; Foreword by Wayne Teasdale
6 x 9, 224 pp, b/w photos, Quality PB, 978-1-893361-35-5 **$16.95**

Lighting the Lamp of Wisdom: A Week Inside a Yoga Ashram
by John Ittner; Foreword by Dr. David Frawley
6 x 9, 192 pp, 10+ b/w photos, Quality PB, 978-1-893361-52-2 **$15.95**

Making a Heart for God: A Week Inside a Catholic Monastery
by Dianne Aprile; Foreword by Brother Patrick Hart, OCSO
6 x 9, 224 pp, b/w photos, Quality PB, 978-1-893361-49-2 **$16.95**

Waking Up: A Week Inside a Zen Monastery
by Jack Maguire; Foreword by John Daido Loori, Roshi
6 x 9, 224 pp, b/w photos, Quality PB, 978-1-893361-55-3 **$16.95**; HC, 978-1-893361-13-3 **$21.95**

Judaism / Christianity / Interfaith

Talking about God: Exploring the Meaning of Religious Life with Kierkegaard, Buber, Tillich and Heschel *by Daniel F. Polish, PhD*
Examines the meaning of the human religious experience with the greatest theologians of modern times.   6 x 9, 176 pp, HC, 978-1-59473-230-0 **$21.99**

Interactive Faith: The Essential Interreligious Community-Building Handbook
Edited by Rev. Bud Heckman with Rori Picker Neiss
A guide to the key methods and resources of the interfaith movement.
6 x 9, 304 pp, HC, 978-1-59473-237-9 **$40.00**

The Jewish Approach to Repairing the World (*Tikkun Olam*)
A Brief Introduction for Christians *by Rabbi Elliot N. Dorff, PhD, with Reverend Cory Willson*
A window into the Jewish idea of responsibility to care for the world.
5½ x 8½, 256 pp, Quality PB, 978-1-58023-349-1 **$16.99** (a Jewish Lights book)

Modern Jews Engage the New Testament: Enhancing Jewish Well-Being in a Christian Environment *by Rabbi Michael J. Cook, PhD*
A look at the dynamics of the New Testament.
6 x 9, 416 pp, HC, 978-1-58023-313-2 **$29.99** (a Jewish Lights book)

Disaster Spiritual Care: Practical Clergy Responses to Community, Regional and National Tragedy
Edited by Rabbi Stephen B. Roberts, BCJC, & Rev. Willard W.C. Ashley, Sr., DMin, DH
The definitive reference for pastoral caregivers of all faiths involved in disaster response.
6 x 9, 384 pp, Hardcover, 978-1-59473-240-9 **$40.00**

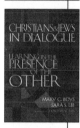

The Changing Christian World: A Brief Introduction for Jews
by Rabbi Leonard A. Schoolman
5½ x 8½, 176 pp, Quality PB, 978-1-58023-344-6 **$16.99** (a Jewish Lights book)

The Jewish Connection to Israel, the Promised Land: A Brief Introduction for Christians *by Rabbi Eugene Korn, PhD*
5½ x 8½, 192 pp, Quality PB, 978-1-58023-318-7 **$14.99** (a Jewish Lights book)

Christians and Jews in Dialogue: Learning in the Presence of the Other
by Mary C. Boys and Sara S. Lee; Foreword by Dorothy C. Bass
Inspires renewed commitment to dialogue between religious traditions.
6 x 9, 240 pp, HC, 978-1-59473-144-0 **$21.99**

Healing the Jewish-Christian Rift: Growing Beyond Our Wounded History
by Ron Miller and Laura Bernstein; Foreword by Dr. Beatrice Bruteau
6 x 9, 288 pp, Quality PB, 978-1-59473-139-6 **$18.99**

Introducing My Faith and My Community
The Jewish Outreach Institute Guide for the Christian in a Jewish Interfaith Relationship
by Rabbi Kerry M. Olitzky 6 x 9, 176 pp, Quality PB, 978-1-58023-192-3 **$16.99** *(a Jewish Lights book)*

The Jewish Approach to God: A Brief Introduction for Christians
by Rabbi Neil Gillman 5½ x 8½, 192 pp, Quality PB, 978-1-58023-190-9 **$16.95** *(a Jewish Lights book)*

Jewish Holidays: A Brief Introduction for Christians
by Rabbi Kerry M. Olitzky and Rabbi Daniel Judson
5½ x 8½, 176 pp, Quality PB, 978-1-58023-302-6 **$16.99** *(a Jewish Lights book)*

Jewish Ritual: A Brief Introduction for Christians
by Rabbi Kerry M. Olitzky and Rabbi Daniel Judson
5½ x 8½, 144 pp, Quality PB, 978-1-58023-210-4 **$14.99** *(a Jewish Lights book)*

Jewish Spirituality: A Brief Introduction for Christians *by Rabbi Lawrence Kushner*
5½ x 8½, 112 pp, Quality PB, 978-1-58023-150-3 **$12.95** *(a Jewish Lights book)*

A Jewish Understanding of the New Testament
by Rabbi Samuel Sandmel; new Preface by Rabbi David Sandmel
5½ x 8½, 368 pp, Quality PB, 978-1-59473-048-1 **$19.99**

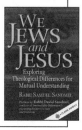

We Jews and Jesus: Exploring Theological Differences for Mutual Understanding
by Rabbi Samuel Sandmel; new Preface by Rabbi David Sandmel A Classic Reprint
6 x 9, 192 pp, Quality PB, 978-1-59473-208-9 **$16.99**

Show Me Your Way: The Complete Guide to Exploring Interfaith Spiritual Direction
by Howard A. Addison 5½ x 8½, 240 pp, Quality PB, 978-1-893361-41-6 **$16.95**

About SKYLIGHT PATHS Publishing

SkyLight Paths Publishing is creating a place where people of different spiritual traditions come together for challenge and inspiration, a place where we can help each other understand the mystery that lies at the heart of our existence.

Through spirituality, our religious beliefs are increasingly becoming a part of our lives—rather than *apart* from our lives. While many of us may be more interested than ever in spiritual growth, we may be less firmly planted in traditional religion. Yet, we do want to deepen our relationship to the sacred, to learn from our own as well as from other faith traditions, and to practice in new ways.

SkyLight Paths sees both believers and seekers as a community that increasingly transcends traditional boundaries of religion and denomination—people wanting to learn from each other, *walking together, finding the way.*

For your information and convenience, at the back of this book we have provided a list of other SkyLight Paths books you might find interesting and useful. They cover the following subjects:

Buddhism / Zen	Global Spiritual	Monasticism
Catholicism	Perspectives	Mysticism
Children's Books	Gnosticism	Poetry
Christianity	Hinduism /	Prayer
Comparative	Vedanta	Religious Etiquette
Religion	Inspiration	Retirement
Current Events	Islam / Sufism	Spiritual Biography
Earth-Based	Judaism	Spiritual Direction
Spirituality	Kabbalah	Spirituality
Enneagram	Meditation	Women's Interest
	Midrash Fiction	Worship

Or phone, fax, mail or e-mail to: SKYLIGHT PATHS Publishing
Sunset Farm Offices, Route 4 • P.O. Box 237 • Woodstock, Vermont 05091
Tel: (802) 457-4000 • Fax: (802) 457-4004 • www.skylightpaths.com
Credit card orders: (800) 962-4544 (8:30AM–5:30PM ET Monday–Friday)
Generous discounts on quantity orders. SATISFACTION GUARANTEED. Prices subject to change.